Molière

.

DON JUAN

Praise For The Molière/Wadsworth Don Juan

Stephen Wadsworth's translation of Don Juan *is not only a brilliant restoration of Molière's original text; it also carries a prophetic message for today. As we watch the hero mercilessly demolishing the myths, dogmas and idols of 17th- century France, pushing the ancien régime into the Enlightenment, we become uncomfortably aware of the hypocrisy, complacency and irrationality of our own time. Socrates insisted that every one of our received ideas and values be subjected to stringent scrutiny. Molière attempted this for his own nation at a time of painful transition; Stephen Wadsworth is asking us to do this at another pivotal and frightening period of historical change.*

Karen Armstrong
Fields of Blood: Religion and the History of Violence; A History of God

An amazing, and utterly fascinating, work of historical reconstruction. Highly relevant to current debates—and lots of fun.

Cass R. Sunstein
Why Societies Need Dissent; Laws of Fear: Risk and Reason

Molière's suppressed text emerges from Stephen Wadsworth's fierce reimagining as a free-wheeling road movie in which master and servant barrel through the treacherous landscape of 17th-century Europe, questioning everything in their path. This Don Juan *reads like a seminal text on church and state, the division of wealth, class friction, and free speech at its most enlightening and dangerous— i.e. many of the hot-button issues of American life today. Virtuoso writing and* funny.

Anna Deavere Smith
Notes from the Field; Let Me Down Easy; Twilight: Los Angeles, 1992

Molière

·

DON JUAN

Translated and Adapted by
Stephen Wadsworth

Great Translations for Actors

A SMITH AND KRAUS BOOK

Molière: DON JUAN Copyright © 2002, 2014, 2017 by Stephen Wadsworth Zinsser

ISBN 9781575259017
Library of Congress Control Number: 2015950761

Cover Photos by: T. Charles Erickson
Interior Photos by: T. Charles Erickson
Typesetting, layout and design by Elizabeth Monteleone

All photographs by T. Charles Erickson, by arrangement with the photographer.

For Joan DeJean

*Historical sense and poetic sense should not,
in the end, be contradictory.*

Robert Penn Warren

*And so the asking of questions and the relating of
narrative need not, I think, be mutually exclusive
forms of historical representation.*

Simon Schama

TABLE OF CONTENTS

This book invites the reader to consider the history of Molière's much-censored and oft-bowdlerized play *Don Juan*, and to imagine, through this version of its text, its original fire.

The received text of *Don Juan,* we know, cannot simply be called Molière's. So many people had cut, stripped, misreported, buried and rewritten Molière's original that by its eighteenth year it was already shrouded in mystery. I now join the ranks of the tinkerers, thereby possibly further confusing the issue of authenticity, but with the intention of making the scope of this play's achievement evident to reader, auditor and interpreter, and of restoring a broken art work with its creator's intentions in mind. Molière's wildly controversial script enjoyed exactly one performance before the censors and lobbyists started pulling it apart. This version supposes what could or might have been heard that night, and means to bring modern audiences into the hour of the play's premiere— the high stakes for all involved, and the alarming effect the text and its ideas clearly had on those present.

There is much of *Don Juan* about which we can only suppose, starting with the title itself. Those who speak of the play in the 17th century, even after Molière's death, always refer to the work he staged in 1665 as *Le Festin de pierre*; they never use the title we now take for granted. In all other languages into which *Don Juan* was transferred, the title is translated as *The Stone Guest*; no one knows why in French alone it became the stone "feast" (*festin*). Some commentators speculate that it was understood that the guest at the banquet would be a statue of the gentleman killed by Molière's hero before the play's action begins. *Pierre* means "stone" in French, hence "the feast of stone." Some point out that the dead gentleman was sometimes called Don Pierre.

This book includes a brief history of the play's suppression and early published editions, by Joan DeJean, an indefatigable scholar of Molière, *Don Juan*, and French culture. It also includes a brief chapter about Molière's political and theatrical milieu, and a conversation between me and Janice Paran, my dramaturg and editor on this adaptation, about how I fell into step with *Don Juan* and what I discovered in its company. We touch on the burgeoning Enlightenment, Molière's literary personality, his relationship with Louis XIV and the politics of the court, his great trilogy of masterpieces, theatrical style in 17th-century Paris and in America today, as well as this version of *Don Juan*. I have also included bits of two contemporary documents in an appendix, and a pronunciation guide.

The informational sections of the book overlap a bit. We hope they will help readers get deeper into the ideas of this play, into Molière's achievement, and perhaps into other glories of baroque art.

Stephen Wadsworth

ERASING *DON JUAN*

Joan DeJean

In theory, we Americans, with our free press and around-the-clock media, are dedicated to airing publicly the events and actions troubling to our society's sense of itself and its mission—and to remembering them. In theory, moreover, we feel a responsibility never to forget them. Yet we know all too well that we rarely know everything, that news is regularly suppressed or manipulated, and that many public-record stories are not made public for years or generations. It was ever thus. Official, state-sponsored censorship has for centuries played a key role in the work of forgetting.

Today, Molière is the central author of the French tradition, and it seems inconceivable that, at the time of its creation, one of the major plays of the most significant period of his career—the play many now refer to as his masterpiece—was made to disappear by the official censors of Louis XIV's France. Those censors intended to erase the play permanently, but fortunately some evidence of their work remains, through which we can catch a glimpse into the public record of 17th-century Paris. That play as Stephen Wadsworth has now translated and adapted it can be thought of as a crucial missing page in the history of French literature. Virtually unknown for the two centuries following its creation, it remains imperfectly known even today. The adaptation you will read in this volume is an important step in the process of remembering a work long covered up, the play we now refer to as *Dom Juan*.[1] And it is an irony that this act of remembering has not occurred in France, which touts *Dom Juan* as one of its seminal classics.

Molière's version of the Don Juan legend was in trouble even before its 1665 opening night. During the entire previous year, he had been embroiled in a struggle that proved to be a founding moment for censorship of the stage in France, the first time that the monarchy is known to have stepped in to suppress a play. On May 12, 1664, Molière presented to Louis XIV and his court the first version of the work we now know as *Le Tartuffe*. His adversaries were waiting for him.

The enemies I have in mind were the members of the Compagnie du Saint-Sacrement, founded in the 1630s and firmly established by mid-century, with branches all over France. The Compagnie was a highly secret religious police, whose members relied on spies to infiltrate all ranks of French society and then used the information thus gathered to enforce their vision of religiously correct thought. The minutes of their April 17, 1664 meeting—nearly a month before Molière staged his new play—record how the members of the Parisian cell had "loudly agreed to work to obtain the suppression of the abominable play *Tartuffe*. Each member undertook to speak to his friends with influence at the court." The Compagnie did its work so thoroughly that, even though its members and their friends in high places did not succeed in preventing the play from being performed in the relatively private setting of Versailles, the King, faced with the uproar they had unleashed, moved quickly to suppress Molière's play.

It was in the course of the summer of 1664, when he was fighting to keep *Le Tartuffe* alive, that Molière began writing a new work. Rather than play it safe, he knowingly jumped right into the lion's mouth and centered his next play on the very subject matter that was bringing the curtain down on the first version of *Le Tartuffe*: the relationships among church, state, and individual human being. *Dom Juan's* saga had begun.

---

[1] In 17th-century French, the Spanish honorific *don* ("sir" or "lord") was more often than not written *dom*: in France this spelling has been maintained with respect to Molière's play.

The history of this long-forgotten play is more than unusually complicated. It begins in Molière's theater in Paris on February 15, 1665, opening night for his company's production of a new play, which he called *Le Festin de pierre*.[2] This performance was the only time that the text as Molière conceived it would ever be heard.

Molière's new play was an instant succès de scandale. He had obviously succeeded in creating a buzz about it before it opened: we know that on opening night, both partisans and enemies of the already controversial author were in the audience, all busily transcribing the text as it was being performed. They undoubtedly had an inkling that this show would not be allowed to go on for long; if so, they were right. Already by the next night's performance, the second scene of the third act, the conversation between the title character and a pauper, had been almost completely removed. It's easy to see why: Don Juan tempts a penniless man to curse God for a gold coin. No one knows who ordered Molière to make this crucial cut; it seems inconceivable, however, given the censorship drama of the previous year, that anyone other than the king would have dared to intervene. Moreover, in August of 1665, six months after the premiere of *Don Juan*, Louis raised Molière's annual pension and took over from his own brother the patronage of Molière's troupe.

Most of what we know about the play as Molière originally conceived it we know thanks to those audience members who were scribbling away madly on opening night. One of them, for example, immediately published a pamphlet attacking the play, reserving his most vehement objections for lines about which he was obliged to add "this line was heard on opening night." Subsequent audiences saw an increasingly censored work.

Molière's company continued to perform its succès de scandale for a little over a month, and the box office receipts prove that it was the biggest hit of his entire career. Thus, it must

---

[2] Those who speak of the play in the 17th century, even after Molière's death, always refer to the work he staged in 1665 as *Le Festin de pierre*; they never use the title we now take for granted. See *Introduction* for further information on the title.

have seemed that the modifications he had made in response to the initial outcry had done the trick. In fact, things were going so well on March 11 that Louis Billaine, one of the publishers with whom Molière worked most regularly, applied for and obtained official, royal permission to publish the play. Only nine days later, on March 20, Molière's theater closed for the Easter holiday, following a performance of its current hit: this was to be the last staging of anything close to Molière's version of the *Don Juan* story for nearly two centuries. When the theater reopened after vacation, *Le Festin de pierre* had simply disappeared. Molière himself never again attempted to stage the play, and Billaine's proposed publication was cancelled.

We may never know how Molière was persuaded to remove *Le Festin de pierre* from the stage. It is impossible to interpret silence and, in the case of Molière's thoughts on this play, silence is all we have as of March 20, 1665. From this point on, we have no record of his ever having mentioned the play again.

In 1673, when Molière died, the suppressed play was still a hot property, and its second life began. Dutch editors, safe from the long arm of French censorship, began a series of attempts to publish it. At first, they were clearly unable to get their hands on a version in any way connected with Molière; they simply published other French versions of the Don Juan legend and used Molière's name on the title page.

Then, in 1677, Molière's widow decided to exploit an untapped part of her inheritance: she provided a manuscript of the play no one had seen for a dozen years to the play-wright Thomas Corneille (Pierre's far less talented younger brother). He produced a new play, also entitled *Le Festin de pierre*, that so thoroughly avoids all the hot-button issues to which the censors had objected that it is truly a travesty of Molière's original. In no time at all, however, the remaining actors from Molière's former company bought the stage rights to Corneille's version and began staging this thoroughly bogus *Le Festin de pierre*.

Amazingly, everyone seemed happy: the contemporary press rushed in to praise the watered-down comedy as "*Le*

Festin de pierre of the famous Molière put into verse by M. Corneille the younger." This is just the confusion that helped pass Corneille's play off for centuries as somehow actually by Molière. Indeed, until the mid-nineteenth century, in France and elsewhere, it continued to be staged instead of any text more closely linked to Molière, despite the fact that more authentic versions of the play became available as early as 1683.

The recovery of Molière's original began in 1682, when the editors of the first edition of Molière's complete works decided to attempt at long last to publish *Le Festin de pierre*. Clearly they were seeking to distance their edition from Molière's sulfurous original—one immediately visible sign is their renaming of the play: *Dom Juan, ou Le Festin de pierre*. In no time at all, the subtitle was dropped, and the play became known simply as *Dom Juan*, a title Molière had never used. The editors made no attempt to include the controversial lines that Molière had been forced to eliminate after opening night. Even so, they were not able to satisfy the censors who, nearly eighteen years after the mutilation of the staged version of the play, were still determined that the work as Molière conceived it should remain forgotten.

The first stroke of good luck encountered by Molière's play proves that this was the case: the volume of the 1682 edition containing *Dom Juan* (volume 7) had already been printed when the censors decided to intervene. They demanded many additional cuts. They also demanded that all the copies already printed be destroyed. However, at least one person decided not to comply fully with that last order, and a few copies of the text as it was originally printed were saved from destruction. Those copies show us why, seventeen years after its premiere, the censors were still unwilling to let the play be remembered.

The biggest problem continued to be the scene with the pauper. The editors originally tried to get a streamlined version of it into print, but the censors rejected even this and reduced the scene to a few lines of meaningless exchange. Then, there was the play's ending. Sganarelle's last speech was completely rewritten: the comic elements—in particular the refrain "my wages, my wages"—were eliminated, and the passage was transformed into a moralizing comment on his master's fate. To complete this process, a lengthy stage direction was added that demonstrates, graphically, nature's satisfaction at the atheist's elimination from this earth: it specifies that thunder and lightning break out and that "flames pour out of the spot where he was engulfed." Once the censors had done their work, no one would have guessed from its ending that the play had been conceived as a comedy.

And that was, of course, the point. Molière had not only dared to bring religious freethinking completely out into the open and to show how it affects his characters' daily lives (master and servant freely discuss Dom Juan's religious beliefs, or rather his lack of them; all his hero's actions are guided by his atheism), but he had made audiences laugh at it all. The 1682 *Dom Juan* eliminated those edgy laughs.

The censors' manhandling of the play provoked one immediate response: someone with a manuscript of the original staged version handed it over to a Dutch publisher, Henri Wetstein, who in 1683 put it into print. This Amsterdam text is without a doubt the most accurate version of the play available; it shows us as much as we can now know about the play as it was staged by Molière. Outside of France, Europe on the verge of the Enlightenment was clearly ready to make a classic of *Le Festin de pierre*: the 1683 text was reedited numerous times in Amsterdam, in Brussels, in Berlin, and in Italy. It became the standard version of the play all over Europe—but not in France.

In France, one process that proved crucial to the fast-developing Enlightenment was already becoming widespread: underground classics were simply printed elsewhere and smuggled across French borders. Molière's play features all the elements one imagines would have guaranteed it status as an Enlightenment classic, from freethinking to class struggles. And yet, mysteriously, there is no evidence that any influential French reader ever came across any of the European editions of *Le Festin de pierre*. Even that crucial

Enlightenment figure Voltaire, who spent so much of his life outside of France, wrote a preface to an edition of *Dom Juan* in which it is clear that he knew that the version he was introducing had been censored and even that he was familiar with some of the content to which the censors had objected—but it is also clear that he is unaware of the content found only in the Amsterdam edition. In France, *Le Festin de pierre* was so successfully covered up that no one could see it, even when it was hidden in plain sight.

The play as Molière conceived it continued to be forgotten all through the eighteenth century and for much of the following century as well. In 1819, some of the long-censored content was at last published in France. However, French theaters continued to stage Thomas Corneille's version rather than Molière's until mid-century. And it was only in 1870 that a French editor finally included, in notes, all the material available only in the edition first published in Amsterdam in 1683. Even today, no edition published in France follows the Dutch text: for each censored scene, editors produce a composite of the various versions. As a result, no two currently available editions of *Dom Juan* are identical.[3]

This is the context in which Stephen Wadsworth's new translation should be viewed. Wadsworth does not follow the Amsterdam edition to the letter: in order to help audiences and readers today understand why this play inspired such stringent official repression, he has amplified or otherwise adapted some elements of the text. But Wadsworth, to my knowledge, is the first translator of Molière's version of the Don Juan legend to work from the Amsterdam edition rather than a censored text, the first translator who has worked to avoid reproducing content for which the censors, rather than Molière, bear the responsibility. This is the first time that an English-speaking audience will be able to approach Molière's play without the smoke screen thrown up by its seventeenth-century censors.

---

[3] The editors of a recent edition of Molière's *Œuvres complètes* state that they follow the 1683 Amsterdam version of the play. However, on numerous occasions they use instead the 1682 French text. See *Œuvres complètes,* ed. Georges Forestier and Claude Bourqui, volume 2. Paris: Gallimard, 2010.

Both Molière and the institution of censorship emerged transformed from their confrontation. Until Molière staged *Le Festin de pierre,* playwrights knew that, on the stage, they could get away with anything—at least once. There was no pre-performance censorship, but there were unwritten rules of self-censorship, which no author before Molière had failed to respect. No one had ever created such a scandal. The authorities were not willing to risk a repeat performance. Soon after, French censors began to adopt the model operative in Elizabethan England, where the chief censor, the Master of the Revels, screened all plays before they were performed. Not long after those explosive years in the 1660s, a "police de théâtres" began keeping a firm rein on the French stage.

Molière emerged chastened from the experience. From then on, he confined his satirical genius to the safer terrain of social manners: witness the example of his next masterpiece, *Le Misanthrope* (1666). True, he was eventually able to perform and to publish a revised version of *Le Tartuffe.* With *Le Festin de pierre,* however, he knew a fate the other great dramatists of his day, Corneille and Racine, could never have imagined. He died thinking that one of the plays from his greatest period had been permanently eliminated from his oeuvre.

It's impossible to imagine how anyone could have made Molière's long repressed play acceptable to any censors. In the case of *Le Tartuffe,* the family bonds together to force the impostor out of their lives; the king guarantees that he will never return to threaten the social order. *Dom Juan*'s contagion cannot, however, be so neatly contained, even by the "cautionary" gesture of a fiery death. In this, his most deeply subversive play, Molière addressed issues of religious and social morality; he also couched them in thoroughly practical terms—Is it acceptable to commit blasphemy if you are starving and someone offers you money on that condition? Do servants serve their masters out of loyalty, or do they care only about their paychecks? By presenting freethinking religious and political views as matters of the pocketbook as much as of conscience, Molière made them seem ordinary, commonplace, unavoidable forces from which no family would ever be safe.

JOAN DEJEAN is Trustee Professor of French at the University of Pennsylvania. She is the author of ten books, including *The Reinvention of Obscenity: Sex, Lies, and Tabloids in Early Modern France* (University of Chicago Press, 2002); *The Essence of Style* (Simon and Schuster, 2005); *The Age of Comfort* (Bloomsbury, 2009); and *How Paris Became Paris: The Invention of the Modern City* (Bloomsbury, 2014). Her edition of Molière's *Dom Juan, ou le Festin de Pierre* was published in 1999 by Droz, Geneva.

CONTEXTUALIZING MOLIÈRE

Stephen Wadsworth

In Politics

Molière's life (1622-1673) started during the reign of Louis XIII (1610-1643) and ended halfway through the reign of Louis XIV (1643-1715). Both kings came to the throne before they were ten years old, and their mothers—both from non-French royal families—ruled as regents until their sons came of age at fourteen. Both queen regents relied principally on brilliant, authoritarian prelates to govern France.

The first, Armand Jean du Plessis de Richelieu (1585-1642), through his wide-ranging initiatives to protect France from invasive neighbors outside and aggressive nobles and non-Catholic elements within, essentially made the gloomy, alienated and cold Louis XIII seem a strong, powerful king.

The second, the Italian-born Jules Mazarin (1602-1661), a disciple of Richelieu, took office at the invitation of Louis XIV's mother, Anne of Austria, with whom he may also have had more than a business relationship. His style was ostensibly more relaxed than Richelieu's, but he was no less ambitious or absolutist in his consolidation of power, for himself as well as for the realm.

Church and state were therefore inseparable in Molière's lifetime. The burgeoning Enlightenment, the emergence of rationalism, began to pry them apart towards the end of the 17th century, and it could be argued that Molière's *Don Juan* influenced that change as much as any scientific or philosophical writing in 17th-century France.

Louis XIV, unlike his father, was charming, robust and independent, and upon attaining his majority made it immediately clear that he and he alone would rule France—not his mother, not a church statesman, not self-interested nobles. Upon hearing that the Parlement, the judiciary body, was meeting without his knowledge, this confident 16-year-old rode directly from the hunt, strode into the chamber in riding boots, and famously intoned, with a crack of his crop, "L'État, c'est moi" (*I* am the government). Louis' proactive style brought many welcome winds of change to France, but the continuing hard-line influence of Catholic zealotry preserved a rather medieval absolutism at the nation's heart and, combined with Louis' weaknesses—for personal glory, grandeur, somewhat indiscriminate sexual dalliances, and later a taste for military aggression—sent contradictory messages of rigor and decadence.

As a merchant-class teenager, Molière would have been aware of the building of the vast Palais-Royal and the development of the marshy islands in the Seine into an exquisite cityscape, both projects overseen by Richelieu. He was probably aware of the near loss of France to Spain and Austria, two constantly nettling neighbors, and of the popular uprising after Richelieu's ruthless tax increases. He was surely aware of the widespread poverty and privation suffered by most of Paris, though he may not have realized that most French people lived as serfs with no property and virtually no rights. And as a young man excited by literature and the theater he was certainly aware of the Académie Française, founded by Richelieu in 1635 to ensure and enshrine the purity of French language and letters, and of the leading playwright of the day, Pierre Corneille (1606-1684), one of the three great playwrights of 17th-century France. The next was to be Molière himself, the third Jean Racine (1639-1699).

The greatest domestic crisis of Louis XIV's France was the civil war of 1648-1653, the *Frondes*, so called for the slingshots used by rebels hostile to Mazarin and the royal family. The situation was this: the Parlement had gradually attempted to limit the growing power of the throne; certain nobles, including the eccentric, ambitious military hero the Prince de Condé, also turned against the royal family for this reason; and the people, miserable under the draconian taxation of the Richelieu-Mazarin economy, had come to the end of their financial tether. The *Frondes* was a series of uprisings of increasing violence. Condé and his imposing sister, Madame de Longueville—cousins of the king, by the way—marched on Paris to seize control; Mazarin secretly fled the country and advised the queen mother from abroad; allegiances to rebels and royals shifted constantly: the young Louis and his mother, in grave danger, fled the city more than once. Paris was a mess—barricaded, embattled, key buildings torched—and in the countryside crops and livestock were destroyed and thousands of peasants were dispossessed. Voltaire later wrote that the people were "a tempest-tossed sea whose waves were driven in all directions by a hundred contrary winds." Needless to say, it was not a golden hour for Parisian theater.

Eventually, in 1652, Mazarin led an army back into town. The crazed derring-do duo, Condé and de Longueville, were trapped and, remarkably, pardoned. And Louis himself returned at the end of the year. With the help of his visionary finance minister Jean Baptiste Colbert, Louis turned the French economy around in the next decade, and launched a new era of achievement in many areas of French government, industry and culture.

•

In Theater

Pierre Corneille created a new dramatic genre, the serious-minded, high-entertainment verse tragedy. These were honor-and-glory plays in extravagant Alexandrine verse, full of spectacle, rhetoric and active heroes caught between ambition and passion.

The 1637 premiere of *Le Cid*, based on a 12th-century Castilian poem about a Spanish hero who fought the Moors, was a red-letter night in French theater history. Corneille's exuberant style pushed at the limits of what the Académie Française considered proper and provoked heated disagreement over what classicism, specifically French classicism, was. The play overflowed the narrow banks of the Academy's rigorous definition but swept up the public with its intensity and recklessness. At the heart of the debate was a conflict between a search for truth and imposed standards of propriety in matters of form, content and, most important, morality, which was the underlying focus of Richelieu's very Catholic original idea of the Academy. Corneille's theater was seen by the Academy to celebrate the moral autonomy of the individual and new expressive reaches for the French language, neither a direction the Academy wished to condone. Corneille's fortunes waxed and waned during the reign of Louis XIV, during which time he had to endure the popularity first of Molière, who occasionally parodied him and must have seemed a scrawny literary talent poaching as he did in the dubious forest of Italian comedy, and then of Jean Racine, whose great tragedies eclipsed his own, and who moreover attacked him in the prefaces to several of them.

Racine's history-making night came in 1667, thirty years after Corneille's (and two years after *Don Juan*). *Andromaque* (Andromache) was the first of his seven great tragedies of the next ten years. Here was lyric tragedy vastly more focused and pared down than Corneille's, less active but psychologically harrowing and full of emotional ambiguity. Racine is very clearly the greater poet, capturing in crisp, ravishing language extremely complex characters, and their destructive passions and long-pondered moral decisions. Racine said he imitated only Euripides and Sophocles; his language certainly has Euripidean flow, and his characters have a sort of Sophoclean density. In form and content Racine's work redefined French classicism. But *Phèdre*, the last and arguably the greatest of the seven tragedies, failed, and Racine, newly married and restored to his Jansenist faith,[4] left the theater for

---

[4] Jansenism, named for its Dutch founder Cornelis Jansen, was a breakaway sect of Catholicism that emerged in the 1640s.

twelve years and became the royal historiographer. Earlier in his career he had found favor with the first of Louis' two foremost mistresses, Madame de Montespan; he ended his career writing two Biblical dramas at the behest of the second, the devout Madame de Maintenon.

By 1643 Molière had abandoned the study of law and a promised career as the *tapissier du Roi* to found a theater troupe with Madeleine Béjart, already established as an actress, and eight would-be actors. They played tragedy in an inauspicious location, and probably none too well until, having run up an unpayable debt, they fled Paris to play the provinces. Even so, the theater was more interesting to Molière than making the king's bed, one of the duties of the *tapissier du Roi* (the job mainly consisted of taking care of the king's furniture, both at home and on the road).

For thirteen years, including the duration of the *Frondes*, the troupe traveled from city to city and patron to patron, gradually refining their craft and business acumen. Molière emerged first as manager, later as the undisputed power in the troupe (with Béjart, who was becoming an important tragic actress). But he was not a leading man for tragedy and only gradually came to cultivate and accept his gift as a *farceur*. His first full-length play, *L'Étourdi* (The Blunderer, 1655), heavily derivative of an Italian *commedia dell'arte* play and other French imitations, coincided with the end of the *Frondes* and featured a huge comic role for Molière himself. His next play, *Le Dépit amoureux* (The Amorous Quarrel, 1656) was more of an ensemble piece, also neo-Italian. It is likely that Molière wrote other plays during this period, including drafts polished for later "premieres" in Paris. By the mid-1650s theater-going Parisians had seen the troupe elsewhere in France and compared it with the best the capital had to offer, and Béjart's gifts in particular were much-heralded. Molière and Béjart both wanted to take the capital and considered various angles of approach.

On October 24, 1658, everything changed. The twenty-year-old Louis XIV was invited by his brother, called Monsieur, to the Salle des Gardes at the old Louvre for a performance by the troupe, of Corneille's *Nicomède*, after which Molière gave a charming speech, part homage to the royal presence and to the host troupe (also in attendance) and part introduction to his little one-act comedy, *Le Docteur amoureux* (The Doctor in Love), which he then performed delightfully. His skill as a comic actor, and the genre itself—a brisk, one-act sort of satyr play—proved fresh and immensely appealing to the assembled company, and Louis ordered the troupe set up in the Great Hall of the Petit-Bourbon, next to the Louvre, under Monsieur's official patronage. As the Troupe du Monsieur, under Molière's leadership, they debuted ten days later, by one account with *L'Étourdi* and *Le Dépit amoureux,* and played alternate nights with the Italian comedians who had been ensconced there since the 1640s. Paris, exhausted by the *Frondes*, was rediscovering comedy.

A year later Molière's next play, *Les Précieuses ridicules* (The Precious Ladies Ridiculed), was an unprecedented success for the troupe and set off another debate about what was appropriate in French theater and letters. The play shocked probably for a number of reasons, certainly because it sharply satirized the wealthy, the fashionable and the established, and because it did so in an undignified, populist, Italian-influenced farce. It was reviled for degrading the purity and purpose of French language and theatrical style, and Molière, once the aspiring tragedian, was established as author as well as comedy star. He had created a new genre, fusing Italian and French traditions, reviving broad comedy, and focusing its considerable subversive energy, for the first time, on the social fabric of France. He spared no one, but the ruling class was unused to such scrutiny, and to being laughed at in public places by other, lower classes. The authorities duly noted that Molière was a morally dangerous writer.

Though the troupe changed venues in 1661 and from 1665 was called the Troupe du Roi (The King's Company), it played together until Molière's death, and beyond. Madeleine Béjart died in 1672. A year later Molière, who had suffered from tuberculosis for some years, collapsed during a performance of *Le Malade imaginaire* (The Imaginary

Invalid) and died later that night. But no last rites for him, as the first two priests called to his house refused to come, and a third arrived too late; the upside of this was that he was never required to renounce his profession—necessary for actors who wanted to receive last rites. Actors were also not allowed burial in hallowed ground, so Molière's wife, Armande Béjart (daughter of Madeleine, that's another story), petitioned Louis XIV to allow a nocturnal burial in a proper cemetery. The church reluctantly consented.

In 1792 Molière's remains were exhumed at the height of the French Revolution—fitting for the author of *Don Juan*—and spent time under guard in a church basement, then a municipal office, then the Museum of French Monuments, where they were lodged in a hero's sarcophagus. His remains, like his plays, were manipulated by various regimes for various reasons. They found their final resting place in the very center of Père Lachaise cemetery in Paris, surrounded by many of the world's greatest writers and artists.

MOLIÈRE

Don Juan

1665

Translated and Adapted by Stephen Wadsworth

•

For Francesca, muse and love

If Galileo had said in verse *that the world moved,*
the Inquisition might have let him alone.

Thomas Hardy

ACTS

The play was written in five prose acts. This adaptation is meant to be played in two acts, the first comprised of Molière's first three acts, the second comprised of Molière's fourth and fifth acts.

CHARACTERS

The Nobles
> DON JUAN
> DON LUIS, Don Juan's father
> DONNA ELVIRA, seduced and abandoned by Don Juan
> DON CARLOS, Donna Elvira's brother
> DON ALONSO, Donna Elvira's brother
> THE STATUE, of a Viceroy, killed by Don Juan

The Servants
> SGANARELLE, Don Juan's manservant
> GUSMAN, Donna Elvira's servant
> LA VIOLETTE, a servant of Don Juan
> RAGOTIN, a servant of Don Juan

Peasants and Tradespeople
> CHARLOTTE
> PIERROT
> MATHURINE
> A PAUPER
> MONSIEUR DIMANCHE

Spirits
> A SPECTER
> DEATH

SETTING

Molière set the play in Sicily. His original production depicted an idealized painted Sicily, but it's highly unlikely he intended to portray Sicily or Sicilians in *Don Juan*. A far-away setting put the ideas of *Don Juan* at a safe remove from the France they so tellingly criticize, and therefore from the censors' grasp—though sadly in this case no such luck.

ORIGINAL PRODUCTIONS

The first performance took place in Paris, in the theater at the Palais-Royal on February 15, 1665. We know little of Molière's original cast other than that he himself played Sganarelle. It is generally assumed that Don Juan was played by Charles Varlet, called La Grange, a 26-year-old regular in Molière's troupe, apparently charming, handsome and usually cast as the young lover. We know more about the scenery, for which the commissioning contract was discovered fairly recently—an elaborate new set of apparently brilliant trompe l'oeil wing-and-border perspectives, and a complicated transformation into the Viceroy's tomb for the first Statue scene.[5] The costume inventory was likewise large, though in all likelihood only a small part of it was actually built for *Don Juan.*

This adaptation was originally produced, by Seattle Repertory Theatre and the McCarter Theatre in Princeton, N.J., in the Bagley Wright Theater in Seattle, on March 18, 2002, with the following cast and creative contributors (note doublings and triplings, they may be helpful):

PROLOGUE PLAYER	Frank Corrado
GUSMAN	Gilbert Cruz
SGANARELLE	Cameron Folmar
DON JUAN	Adam Stein
DONNA ELVIRA	Francesca Faridany
CHARLOTTE	Mary Bacon
PIERROT	Burton Curtis
MATHURINE	Laura Kenny
LA RAMÉE	Bruce Turk
PAUPER	Burton Curtis
DON CARLOS	Bruce Turk
DON ALONSO	Francesca Faridany

[5] See Appendix 1

STATUE	Gilbert Cruz
LA VIOLETTE	Burton Curtis
MONSIEUR DIMANCHE	Laura Kenny
RAGOTIN	Mary Bacon
DON LUIS	Frank Corrado
SPECTER	Cleopatra Bertelsen
DEATH	Bruce Turk

Director	Stephen Wadsworth
Set Designer	Kevin Rupnik
Costume Designer	Anna Oliver
Lighting Designer	Amy Appleyard
Choreographer	Daniel Pelzig
Fight Director	Geoffrey Alm
Production Stage Manager	Joseph Smelser
Voice and Speech Coach	Kate Wilson
Artistic Director, Seattle Repertory Theatre	Sharon Ott
Artistic Director, McCarter Theatre	Emily Mann
Staff Producer, McCarter Theatre	Mara Isaacs
Dramaturgs	Janice Paran
	Christine Sumption

PROLOGUE

*(The senior actor comes forward to the edge of the
stage. As he speaks he refers occasionally to the
royal box—at the front center of the first balcony.
The company is visible at the sides of the stage.)*

Long live the King! Mesdames, Messieurs, a rousing
    chorus—
Come, salute the gorgeous monarch now before us.
Long live the King, the boldest forward-looking man
To grace the Cath'lic throne of France since France
    began.
Long live the King, the patron saint of all our hopes,
A king from God descended, cousin to the popes.
A king who's learned to exercise his kingly force
In spades, but never fails to exercise his horse.
A king whose loves include affairs...of church and
    state,
Affairs of trade, of war, and...what is on his plate!
United with the church, with God, against transgressors,
He shares the royal secrets only with confessors,
And with them governs ev'ry aspect of finance—
And yet he patronizes playwrights! And can dance!
Long live a king who rules both firmly and with style!
A man of moral rigor, yes, but total lack of guile,
Who knows a hypocrite at sight and wants a friend
To speak his mind and know that he will not offend,
Who by prizing candor honors truth and fosters
Learning, stimulates debate and shames impostors.
Is it only thirty years since Galileo irked the Pope?
Why, no such inquisitions here, no rope
For *French* philosophers and scientists who grope
For unknown essences with ink or telescope.
Long live a king who subsidizes ev'ry form
Of art as well, and weathers ev'ry storm
Of criticism for a painting here, a garden

There, and books and buildings everywhere. He'll pardon
Any artisan who, working in a passion,
Might exceed the limits of accepted fashion.
He pardoned us, we played *Tartuffe*, a comic drama
Telling of a sneaky priest. Its ev'ry comma
Was debated by offended men of God.
The play was meant to work as a divining rod
To find and uproot all the falsity around us,
Not to denigrate true faith, and yet they found us
In contempt. The King then kindly asked that we...
Not play that now incendiary property.
So we shall play *Don Juan*, which we've made...
     crude,
So that, unlike *Tartuffe*, it can't be misconstrued.
Verse begone, begone the unities of time
And place and action. No prevaricating rhyme,
Contemporary characters or subtle plot.
Instead, a fiction drawn from legend, this is *not*
A tale of anyone whom we would ever know,
It's just a bright parade of colorful tableaux.
Our play is nothing next to buildings by LeVau,
Nothing next to paintings by Le Brun, aglow
With rev'rence, nothing next to great Le Nôtre's hoe,
Which tills the gardens of Versailles. And yet we owe
The best of our ebullient craft, however bland,
To our young king, who's favored us so often. *And*—
In case we *do* disturb the beast of politics,
In ev'ry costume we've a hidden crucifix.

     (He takes a crucifix from a pocket.)

Long live the King!

     *(He exits. As the company disperses offstage.
     Transformation to Act I.)*

SCENE 1

(Sganarelle enters, pursued by Gusman.)

GUSMAN

Alas Sganarelle, Sganarelle! You must tell me why you departed so suddenly and with no explanation. My mistress has suffered a terrible blow. It isn't right! Why did you leave, where is Don Juan?

SGANARELLE

(Turning abruptly to the audience and changing the subject) Whatever Aristotle may have thought, whatever the history of philosophy may have concluded about the meaning of life, there's a lot to be said for snuff. It is the passion of all the rich people, the respectable and virtuous people, and he who lives without it frankly doesn't deserve to live.

(He snuffs a pinch.)

A little pinch of tobacco snuffed into the nostrils, where for a suspense-filled moment it addles the senses, can provide much-needed release...

(He sneezes.)

...from all our worldly woes.

GUSMAN

But I...

SGANARELLE

(Interrupts but continues to the audience) Yes yes, you will say that it's hotly debated, that there are the laws and regulations, but I believe that not only does it cleanse the mind...

(He sneezes.)

...of dangerous humors, it actually inspires the soul to virtue, and one actually learns through using it to become, and remain, a respectable man. So snuff is very useful for people like us who were not born to respectability. Surely you've noticed that when you take it yourself, you start to share it, you become suddenly generous and dole it out left and right, wherever you go, whoever the takers. And you certainly don't have to wait for them to ask for it, either, for in offering it you have anticipated everyone's true wish—to be rich, virtuous and respectable!

(He snuffs a pinch.)

Snuff is contagious, it brings all men together...which is probably why there are laws regulating its use!

(He sneezes.)

Ah, tobacco. No wonder the King is so interested in the new world.

(He sneezes.)

(An offering to the royal box) Long live the King!

GUSMAN
Sganarelle—

SGANARELLE
(Interrupts, turns to Gusman) But enough of this frivolous topic, and back to the matter that concerns us. Very well then, we know that your mistress, surprised by our departure, took to the fields in pursuit of us, indeed her heart, which my master had touched so deeply, could not—being so touched—do otherwise.
(A beat.)

Do you want me to tell you what I'm thinking? Just
entre nous? I'm afraid that Donna Elvira will be poorly
rewarded for her love, that her journey to this town will
bear little fruit, and that you would have accomplished
just as much by staying home.

GUSMAN
But tell me, I beg you, what could prompt you to such
a grim reckoning? What is behind it? Has your master
opened his heart to you about this? Has he mentioned
some reason—some unintended offense perhaps which
forced his indifference and compelled him to depart?

SGANARELLE
No, he hasn't. I wish he had. But I pretty much know the
lay of the land, as it were, and although he hasn't yet said a
thing about it to me, I'd almost bet my wages the marriage is
over—if he ever pays me my wages. I could perhaps be mis-
taken, but honestly, experience has taught me a thing or two.

GUSMAN
Over? But such a departure would constitute the breaking of an oath, a law, a trust! Could he do this injury to
Donna Elvira, whose love for him is so pure? A man of
his station, a gentleman, a man of quality and honor, a
man so highly placed at court could do something so
mean-spirited and shameful?

SGANARELLE
Oh yes, he's a man of quality and honor, so there must
be a good reason why he always breaks his word.

GUSMAN
But the vows of marriage bind him, sacred before God!

SGANARELLE
Ah my poor Gusman. My friend, believe me, you don't
yet know what kind of man he is.

GUSMAN

I really don't know what kind of man he *can* be if he can do what he did to us—this treacherous thing. And I don't understand at all how after such a show of impatience, such urgent attentions, such oaths and sighs and tears, such impassioned letters, ardent protestations, repeated declarations, such a frenzy of love—for Heaven's sake he *did* these things! To the point of crossing, in his passion, the sacred threshold of a *convent*, to draw Donna Elvira out and into his power. I'm telling you, I have a great deal of trouble understanding how after all that he could have the heart to break his word to her.

SGANARELLE

Well I don't have any trouble at all understanding. And if you knew our little pilgrim yourself, you'd realize how easy it all is for him. I'm not saying that his feelings for your mistress have changed, I'm still not at all sure they have, I'm just saying that he is not governed by such considerations. He ordered me gone before he left you, and since his arrival here he has said nothing about it I promise you, but I must caution you that in my master, Don Juan, we have the single most vile miscreant the world has ever produced: a dangerous man, a dog, a demon, an infidel, a heretic, who believes in nothing you revere or fear—not Heaven, not saints, not God, not the Devil, Hell or werewolves; who delights in challenging your most cherished beliefs, and lives to prove their folly in actions more lawless and licentious than anything you dare imagine; who is spending this lifetime as a hedonist pig, a pleasure-seeking, pain-avoiding predator as whimsical as Epicurus, as debauched as Sardanapalus but much deafer to all Christian remonstrances than any Muslim zealot could ever be.

You tell me he married your mistress. Be assured that he did it to satisfy his lust, and that if his lust had dictated it he also would have married you, along with her. And her dog. And her cat. Marriage costs him nothing to propose or to arrange, it is his snare of choice. And he's a very hands-on marrier, too, who always has his left hand on the lady as he seduces her daughter, his right hand on the chambermaid as he gooses the mother abbess, and the wrong hand on the Bible as he swears eternal faith. Nothing's too hot or too cold or too fat or too old for him, and if I told you the names of everyone he's married in every place we've been, we would be here until tomorrow night's performance.

(He looks at Gusman.)

You seem taken aback. You blush at what I've told you, but this is at best a hazy outline of our hero, I'd have to paint for weeks to fill it all in. The wrath of God is sure to catch up with him some day. Suffice it to say that I'd be better off in the Devil's service than in his. He's forced me to witness such horrible things that I wish he were already you know where. It's terrible, I have no choice but to serve him faithfully in spite of what I feel. I am afraid. He has wealth and power, and he can do what he wants, who am I? Although can you imagine—he actually asks me what I think about things! But fear keeps me from telling him. Fear motivates me, and I usually end up encouraging, even applauding the things he does, when in my heart I can't bear them.

(He sees Don Juan approaching.)

There he is, he's back from his walk. We have to stop, listen—I've been very frank and confidential with you, but I think it all came out of my mouth a little too fast. If you were to repeat any of this, and my master were somehow to get wind of it, I want you to know that I would tell him that you had lied, and he'd believe me.

(Gusman moves away as Don Juan enters.)

SCENE 2

DON JUAN
Who was that bending your ear?

SGANARELLE
Monsieur…

DON JUAN
I thought he looked sort of like that servant of Elvira's.

SGANARELLE
I thought he looked a lot like him.

DON JUAN
What, was it really he?

SGANARELLE
He himself, Monsieur.

DON JUAN
And when, pray tell, did he arrive here?

SGANARELLE
Last night, Monsieur.

DON JUAN
And what business brings him here?

SGANARELLE
I'm sure you can imagine what might be troubling him.

DON JUAN
Our departure no doubt.

SGANARELLE
The good fellow is completely humiliated and horrified
by it, and he begged me to tell him why it happened.

DON JUAN

And you said—

SGANARELLE

That you'd told me nothing about it.

DON JUAN

Well what are your thoughts on the matter? Why do you think it happened?

SGANARELLE

Me?

DON JUAN

You.

SGANARELLE

You really want to know what I think?

DON JUAN

I really want to know what you think.

SGANARELLE

I think—and I don't mean to say it's wrong of course— that you have some new love in mind.

DON JUAN

Is that really what you think?

SGANARELLE

Yes.

DON JUAN

Well you're dead right.

SGANARELLE

By God, I certainly know my Don Juan.

DON JUAN

And I must confess that this pretty thing has quite chased
Donna Elvira from my thoughts.

SGANARELLE

Monsieur, your heart is the greatest traveler in the
world—eager to see all the sights and never content to
stay in one place for long.

DON JUAN

You don't think I'm right to let it wander in this way?

SGANARELLE

But Monsieur, it is not my place…

DON JUAN

Speak!

SGANARELLE

Well, undoubtedly you are right, if you feel like letting it
wander, as you would so rightly be the first to say, and I
can't argue against that. But if you didn't feel like letting
it wander, well that would be a different matter.

DON JUAN

What are you getting at?

SGANARELLE

Monsieur, it isn't appropriate for servants to—

DON JUAN

(Interrupts) I have given you the liberty to speak freely,
now tell me what you think, I want to know!

SGANARELLE

In that case Monsieur, I will tell you frankly that I don't ap-
prove of the way you go about these things, and that I find it
really contemptible to love on all sides at once as you do.

DON JUAN

I beg your pardon? You really think that one should tie oneself down to the first thing that captures one's fancy, that one should renounce the living world for it, and that one should never again have eyes for anything else? This notion of being faithful, of priding oneself on the honorable choice but suffering underneath, of embalming oneself forever in a grand passion that's grand only at the beginning, of being dead forever more to all the new and beautiful things that might astonish one—it doesn't make sense. No no, constancy works only for people who don't think. Look, all women have the right to charm us, do they not?

SGANARELLE

Of course.

DON JUAN

Then the advantage the first one has in charming us first shouldn't rob all the others of their rightful opportunity to charm us as well! For my part, beauty ravishes me wherever I find it, and I yield willingly to its delectable violence whenever it finds me. My commitment to one beautiful woman doesn't oblige me to do an injustice to all the others. My eyes are still my own, I see the merits of all of them and render to each the tributes and attentions which are natural to offer—indeed which Mother Nature herself demands we offer. Come what may, I can't keep my heart from loving what is lovable, and when a lovable girl asks for my heart, well—if I had a thousand hearts I'd give her every one.

That moment when passion first stirs has an indescribable charm, don't you think? All the pleasure of love is in that moment of awakening, when new love is born and the world is redefined. How can one not feel a deep contentment in helping to effect this change? In softening by a hundred reverent attentions the heart of a young beauty; in marking one's little victories as the days creep by; in battling, with tears and sighs and promises of bliss, the innocent reserve of a soul loath to surrender her secrets; in breaking down step by step each bastion of resistance with which she protects herself; in melting the scruples to which she's given pride of place; and in coaxing her tenderly to where we have longed to take her. But once one has mastered her there's nothing more to say or lust after—the magical moment of change has come and gone, the peak of passion is scaled, and we are lulled to sleep in the complacency of a love like this if our desires are not allowed to be re-awakened by the irresistible promise of some conquest-to-be.

Nothing is so sweet as overcoming a woman's reluctance, and in this arena I have the ambition of the ancient conquerors, who flew from victory to victory and could not be persuaded to limit their desires. There is nothing—no force, no inducement—that can limit mine: I am compelled to love the whole world, impetuously and unstoppably, and like Alexander the Great I wish there were ever further worlds in which to multiply my amorous conquests!

SGANARELLE

God in Heaven you give a good speech! You certainly know how to go on about a thing, it's like you know it by heart. It's just like when the King speaks.

DON JUAN

Bien touché!

SGANARELLE

(Again to the royal box) Long live the King!

DON JUAN

But what do you have to say about what I said?

SGANARELLE

Oh my, I have a lot to say, but I don't know where to start, because you turn things around so that it seems somehow that you're right, and yet I know that you're not right. Oh, I had the prettiest, most coherent answer ready, and your filibuster has messed it all up. Oh well, forget it, next time I'm going to write it down, then we'll have a proper debate.

DON JUAN

Now there's a plan.

SGANARELLE

But Monsieur...

DON JUAN

What?

SGANARELLE

You gave me permission to speak freely.

DON JUAN

Yes.

SGANARELLE

Would that include telling you that I am just the teeniest bit scandalized by the life you are leading?

DON JUAN

What do you mean? What life am I leading?

SGANARELLE

Oh a very good one. But for example when I see you getting married once a month—

DON JUAN

(Interrupts) I find it very agreeable.

SGANARELLE

Yes, true, I understand that it is extremely agreeable, and very...diverting, and I'm sure I could reconcile myself to

45

it soon enough if there were no bad in it. But Monsieur, to play with the sacred mysteries of Heaven!

DON JUAN

Sacred mysteries of Heaven?

SGANARELLE

Yes Monsieur.

DON JUAN

Heaven and I can settle this, just the two of us, we don't need your help.

SGANARELLE

No by God Monsieur, I have always heard that to make light of Heaven is wicked, and that libertines never meet a good end.

DON JUAN

Libertines!

SGANARELLE

Men who think they're above the law, who lack sufficient respect for these sacred things or who disobey the Commandments—

DON JUAN

(Interrupts) Stop right there you dunce, you *dupe*! How many times have I told you I do not like instructional tirades?

SGANARELLE

But I'm not talking about *you*, God forbid. You know what you're about, and if you don't believe in anything, you have your reasons. It's just that there are certain puny, impudent, impertinent people in this world who are libertines without any justification, who play at being free-thinkers on a whim, and if I had a master like that, I'd look him straight in the eye and tell him flat out, "Do you really dare toy with God like that? Do you not tremble to poke fun, as you do every day, at the most holy and sanctified things? It's all very well for you, mere earthworm that you are, *termite* that you are—" I'm not talking to you, I'm talking to my other, termite master. "—It's all very well for you to go around turning what other men revere into some kind of easy joke, but do you think that because you're a person of refinement, because you have a title, because you have feathers in your hat, gold buttons on your coat, ribbons the color of fire and a big curly blond[6] wig—" I'm not talking to you, I'm still talking to the other fellow. "—Do you think, and look at me when I'm talking to you, do you think that therefore you're smarter than other men, that you're allowed to do exactly as you like with no consequences, and that no one will dare tell you the truth about yourself? Well, you're hearing it from me, your own valet! Sooner or later Heaven punishes ungodly profligates, and the nastier your life, the nastier your death!"

DON JUAN

Stop it!

SGANARELLE

What's the matter?!

DON JUAN

The matter is that we're not talking about this, we're talking about a pretty peasant girl who has captured my heart, and whose charms have drawn me here.

SGANARELLE

But we can't stay here, Monsieur, you killed the Viceroy here just six months ago. Aren't you afraid?

---

[6] "Blond" is exchangeable for brown, black, or red, as per the actor's wig color.

DON JUAN
Afraid? Didn't I kill him?

SGANARELLE
Oh you killed him all right, he couldn't have been more
dead. But duels, Monsieur, are illegal—

DON JUAN
I got a royal pardon for that one.

SGANARELLE
Yes but a royal pardon doesn't perhaps cancel out the
resentment of his relatives and friends.

DON JUAN
(Interrupts) Oh let's not talk about the bad things that
could happen to us, let's think about the things that give
us pleasure. Let's think about this girl, the prettiest little
peasant girl in the world, brought here by her intended
to be wed.

(He discovers his snuff.)

Snuff!

(He snuffs a pinch.)

I caught a glimpse of these two several days ago, and I'd
never seen a couple so content together, or so exuberantly
expressive of their love for each other—the palpable
tenderness and...mutuality of their fervor filled me
with...

(He sneezes.)

...emotion! I was struck to the heart by it, and my love
began in fact as jealousy. It's true, at first I couldn't
bear to see them so happy together, and this vexation

kindled my desire, and I imagined the intense pleasure I'd get from sundering this bond that had so distressed my sensitive heart. But until now all my attempts have proved fruitless, and I'm down to a last resort—the would-be-husband means to amuse the fiancée with a promenade *sur mer*.

SGANARELLE
(Aside, to the audience) A boatride.

DON JUAN
Now without troubling you about it I have readied everything for the fulfillment of my desire. I have a sailboat, and a crew, and I intend to abduct the girl.

SGANARELLE
Ah Monsieur, that is really—

DON JUAN
Change tack!

SGANARELLE
Really…brilliant! And you'll do it as it should be done I know. There is nothing in the world like satisfying one's needs, is there?

DON JUAN
I'm glad we see eye to eye, now get yourself ready. And take care to bring all my weapons, so that—

(He sees Donna Elvira approaching.)

Oh unfortunate encounter! *(To Sganarelle)* Traitor, you didn't tell me she herself was here.

SGANARELLE
Monsieur, you didn't ask me.

DON JUAN

She hasn't even changed her clothes, is she mad? To come here, to visit me, in the same old getup—has she no sense of occasion?

SCENE 3

DONNA ELVIRA

Will you not do me the kindness, Don Juan, of acknowledging me?

(A beat.)

May I at least hope that you will deign to look at me?

DON JUAN

Madame, I admit I am surprised, I wasn't expecting you to come here.

DONNA ELVIRA

Yes, I can imagine you wouldn't expect me to follow you, and I can see that you are surprised—though hardly in the way I had hoped. The way you hold yourself, the way you turn away, convinces me finally of what I've been unwilling to believe. I wonder at my simplicity, at the innocence of my heart, in questioning a betrayal that all appearances should have confirmed to me long before this moment. I was credulous enough, I confess it, or rather foolish enough to try to deceive myself, to deny my eyes and my judgment. I've wracked my brain for ways to excuse the unexpected languishing of your affection for me. I've conjured up a hundred legitimate reasons for such a sudden departure, to justify the crime of which my reason accused you. I have rejected any voice that found you guilty and welcomed with pleasure the thousand ephemeral fancies that declared you innocent. But in the end this meeting erases every doubt: the look in your eye has told me everything I struggled so hard not to know. Even so, I would be much relieved to hear from your own lips the reason for your disappearance.

(A beat.)

Pray speak, Don Juan, let us hear how you will justify yourself.

DON JUAN
Madame...Sganarelle here...would be glad to tell you why I disappeared.

SGANARELLE
(Aside, to Don Juan) Me, Monsieur? I don't know anything about it thank you very much.

DONNA ELVIRA
Well then Sganarelle, speak.

DON JUAN
Go on Sganarelle, tell Madame!

SGANARELLE
(Aside, to Don Juan) What should I tell her?!

DONNA ELVIRA
(Misunderstanding Sganarelle's hesitancy) You may approach me, since your master wishes it. Tell me why he left.

DON JUAN
(To Sganarelle) You won't answer?

SGANARELLE
(Aside, to Don Juan) I have nothing to answer with. You're making a mockery of me.

DON JUAN
Answer I tell you!

DONNA ELVIRA

Tell me!

DON JUAN

Do as she says!

DONNA ELVIRA
(To Don Juan) Tell him to answer me.

DON JUAN

Answer her!

DONNA ELVIRA

Please!

SGANARELLE

Madame—

DONNA ELVIRA

Yes?

SGANARELLE

Monsieur—

DON JUAN

Now!

DONNA ELVIRA

Tell me!

SGANARELLE

Madame...

(Don Juan starts to tiptoe away as Elvira listens to Sganarelle.)

Alexander the Great. The ancient conquerors. Flying from victory to victory. These are the reasons for our departure.

(Donna Elvira turns to Don Juan before he can escape.)

DONNA ELVIRA
Would you kindly explain these mysteries?

DON JUAN
Madame. To tell you the truth...

(A beat.)

DONNA ELVIRA
For a gentleman and courtier who is clearly well accustomed to these kinds of situations, you are strangely defenseless. I see you are troubled, I pity you. Why don't you protect yourself with your usual reckless effrontery? Why don't you protest to me that you still and always have the same feelings for me, that you love me yet, and more than ever before, that death alone could part us? Why don't you tell me that a matter of gravest urgency obliged you to leave without warning me, that so pressing was your business that in spite of your best efforts you could neither send word nor get away for some time; that I have only to return home, reassured that you will follow me as soon as possible, since it is a certainty that you burn to rejoin me; and that without me you suffer as a body suffers when it is separated from its soul? That is how you should defend yourself, and yet you stand there confounded and ashamed.

DON JUAN
I can say only, Madame, that I have no talent for lying. I have a sincere heart. I will not say that I still and always have the same feelings for you, or that I burn to rejoin you, because the truth is that I left you only to flee from you—though not at all for the reasons you have imagined, rather for reasons of conscience. It is a question of morality, of scruples: I left because I believe it

would have been a sin to stay with you for one moment
longer. My eyes were opened, my soul came to see that
in marrying you I had stolen you from the seclusion of a
convent, that you had broken vows that committed you
first to something far greater than me, and that Heaven
is the most possessive lover of all. I came to see that our
marriage was nothing but a sort of adultery in disguise,
that it was bound to incur the displeasure of Heaven, and
that ultimately I had no choice but to try to forget you,
and leave you free to return to your real marriage. I was
seized with regret, and I fear God's wrath. Would you
wish, Madame, to contest reasoning so pious, or to have
my damnation on your hands, as you surely would if I
held on to you? For as I'm sure you can see—

DONNA ELVIRA

(Interrupts) Ah you scoundrel, now I see you in your
true colors, and alas for me, too late. But know that your
crime will not go unpunished, and that the same Heaven
with which you make sport must inevitably avenge me
for your treachery.

DON JUAN

Sganarelle, she said "Heaven!"

SGANARELLE

She sure did. But we just laugh that off around here.

DON JUAN

Madame—

DONNA ELVIRA

(Interrupts) Enough. I don't want to hear any more, and
I have only myself to blame for listening this long. Why
do I stand here and demand that you spell out my shame
over and over? Am I a coward? I ought to have drawn
the line at your first word. Look at me now.

(Don Juan looks at Donna Elvira.)

Do not hope that I'll exhaust my indignation in reproaches and abuse—no, it will fire my revenge. False man, Heaven will punish you for violating me—and if Heaven holds no terrors for you, then fear the power of a woman's anger.

(Donna Elvira leaves. Don Juan seems thoughtful.)

SGANARELLE
(Aside) If remorse might just touch his heart…

DON JUAN
(Deep in thought) We must think about how best to resolve this matter.

(He looks at Sganarelle.)

This matter, that is…of the pretty peasant girl.

SGANARELLE
(Shocked and appalled) Ah—

DON JUAN
(Rushing away) To the boat!

SGANARELLE
Oh, what a despicable man it is given me to serve!

(Sganarelle follows Don Juan. Transformation to Act II as Pierrot and Charlotte rush on.)

ACT TWO

SCENE 1

CHARLOTTE

Mother of God, Pierrot, you got there just in the nick
of time!

PIERROT

By all that's sacred, they came this close to getting
sucked under.

CHARLOTTE

So the morning wind blew up and knocked 'em over?

PIERROT

Look Charlotte, I'll tell you how it was, God's honest
truth, so here goes. I was the first to spot 'em, the first to
spot 'em I was. Put short, we're on the shore, me and Fat
Poky, and we're throwing dirtballs at each other, 'cause
you know how Fat Poky likes throwing dirtballs, and me
too, sometimes I like throwing 'em too, anyway we're
cutting up, 'cause there's up to be cut, and I spot something far away flopping around in the water and kind of
lurching towards us. So I look at it real hard and suddenly
I see that I can't see it any more, and I go "Hey Poky, I
think there's some gentlemen swimming out there," so
he goes "Right, you're seeing things 'cause you saw a
cat dic," so I go "By the blood of our Lord Jesus I can
see fine, there's men out there!" "Oh no there isn't," he
goes, "sun's in your eyes." "Oh no it isn't," I go, "Want
to bet?" I go. "Want to bet that it's not my eyes," I go,
"and that they're men," I go, "and that they're swimming right toward us?" "God's death," he goes, "Sure
I'll bet 'cause they aren't!" "Oh yeah?" I go, "want to
bet a penny they are?"

CHARLOTTE

A *penny*!

PIERROT

So he goes "Here's the first penny I ever owned on it, that's how sure I am." That seemed like a lot, but I was sure, so I got all my pieces out like a man, even my little piece with the fleur de lys on it, so it all made up a penny, and God be damned I put that money down as if I'd gulped down a bucket of beer, 'cause I'm plucky, I can take a risk, you think I didn't know what I was about but I did, and anyway as soon as we put down our pieces I see the two men plain as day, making signs for us to go and save 'em, but now I'm thinking I should take the money first. So I go, "Ha ha fat boy, you see 'em calling to us, let's go save 'em," and he goes, "No, they made me lose!" So he's going on like that, and I'm yelling at him, and there's money lying there, and men drowning, and well, to cut it short: I yelled at him so hard that we got us a boat and paddled out there with the waves all topsy-turvy, and we pulled 'em out of the water, two of 'em, and rich, and we took 'em to Mathurine's house and met up with two more of 'em with the stripey jackets all wet and put 'em by the fire, and then they all four of 'em stripped naked...

(Charlotte gasps.)

...to get dry. And then Mathurine got there, and one of 'em starts right in on her, my goodness yes, and she liked that fine, and that's it, Charlotte, that's just how it happened.

CHARLOTTE

Pierrot, were they *all* naked?

PIERROT

They sure were, and the master, he must be some big big Monsieur 'cause he had gold buttons all up and down his coat, top to bottom, and even his servants must be masters 'cause they have the stockings and stripes and silk pants. He may be a big Monsieur, but he would've been sucked under if I hadn't been there!

CHARLOTTE

Well look at *you*!

PIERROT

(Spreading his money out) And here's the two pennies'
worth.

CHARLOTTE

Well look at *that*!

PIERROT

Yes by God, he just about bought the farm, but we saved
him.

CHARLOTTE

Is he still all naked?

PIERROT

(Shaking his head no) Uh-uh, they dried off a while,
'cause there was off to be dried, and he got dry first 'cause
Mathurine helped him a lot. Then they got dressed again
and God's buttons I never saw such dressing up as these
Monsieurs do, what trifles and ornaments and doodads
these courtier types pile on, I'd be lost trying to figure it
all out, I was gauping at it. I mean Charlotte they have hair
that they can take right out of their heads, they just take
it out and put it back in like a great big hat made of flax,
except that they put a real hat on top of it. They have shirts
with arms so big you and me could just walk right into 'em
and disappear, and instead of pants they wear more like
bloomers with enough cloth to stretch from here to Easter
Sunday, and instead of doublets they got teeny little coat
things that hardly come down to their nipples! And instead
of a neckband he's got a huge lacy handkerchief the size
of France with four fat fancy bows marching down to his
belly, and they've got so many ribbons all over them on
their shoes and their heads and their knees and their tails
and their ears, so many layers of linen and silk and cotton

and wool that it's, well, stupid. There's nothing on him, down to his toes, that isn't stuffed and twisted and just so big that I'd trip right over it and break my neck, right down to my bum crack.

CHARLOTTE
Oh Pierrot!

PIERROT
You know who he looks like, he looks like the King in all those stupid clothes.

CHARLOTTE
I want to see this!

PIERROT
(A tentative offering to the royal box) Long live the King.

CHARLOTTE
(Starting off) I'm going to go look at him.

PIERROT
Wait a minute Charlotte, 'cause I have something else to say to you.

CHARLOTTE
Well go ahead and say it then.

PIERROT
Well you see Charlotte, I have to like they say uncork my heart like a bottle. I love you...

> *(Charlotte turns to look at him, and they both stand still.)*

...and you know it, and I want us to get married, but— God's death, I'm not satisfied with you.

CHARLOTTE
What? What's going on with you?

PIERROT
It's…well, you make me lose my temper, that's what's going on.

CHARLOTTE
But how?

PIERROT
God's head, you just don't love me.

CHARLOTTE
Oh is *that* all!

PIERROT
Well it's enough!

CHARLOTTE
God above, Pierrot, you always tell me the same thing.

PIERROT
I always tell you the same thing 'cause it's always the same thing to tell, and if it wasn't the same thing it wouldn't always be the same thing I was telling you!

CHARLOTTE
But what do you *want*, Pierrot?!

PIERROT
God damn you, I want you to love me!

CHARLOTTE
So I don't love you?

PIERROT
No you don't, and I do everything I can to make you. I

buy your ribbons and don't complain, I climb trees and break my neck to bring you pretty blackbirds' nests, I make the fiddlers fiddle on your name day, but it's like banging my head against a wall. It's just not right or fair to not love people who love us!

CHARLOTTE

But Christ on the cross, I *do* love you!

PIERROT

But you love me so *badly*!

CHARLOTTE

Well what do you want me to do about it?!

PIERROT

I want you to love me the way you're supposed to.

CHARLOTTE

I don't love you the way you're supposed to?

PIERROT

No! 'cause if you did, everybody could see it, 'cause you're always playing little tricks on people when you love them with all your heart. Look at Tomasina, she's head over heels for Fat Poky, she never lets him alone, she's always playing some joke or giving him a good smack when she passes him, and the other day he was sitting on a stool and she pulled it right out from under his bum and made him fall flat out on the ground, now *that's* what people do who love you, but you just stand there like a post, and I'd go by you twenty times before you'd smack me!

CHARLOTTE

Well that's just my way, I can't melt myself down and make myself over.

PIERROT

Well it's no way to be—when you like someone specially you have to really let 'em know it, everybody does *that*.

CHARLOTTE

All right then, I really love you as much as I can. If you're not satisfied with me, I guess you'll have to go love some other person!

PIERROT

Oh that's *just* what I wanted! God's *feet*, would you say that if you loved me?!

CHARLOTTE

Why do you always bother me and make me sad?!

PIERROT

Ha! So I'm bothering *you*, I'm making *you* sad, God's *bum*!

(A beat.)

I'm just asking for a little more affection.

CHARLOTTE

Well take it easy then, and don't push me so much, and maybe it will just happen, without always talking about it.

PIERROT

(Offering his hand) Put it there, Charlotte.

CHARLOTTE

(Offering hers) All right, there.

PIERROT

(Bending near to her) Promise you'll try to love me more.

CHARLOTTE
(Bending near to him) I'll do the best I can, but it has to come on its own.

(They kiss. Charlotte knocks Pierrot down.)

PIERROT
(A joyful announcement) She knocked me down!

CHARLOTTE
I'll meet you at the church, Pierrot!

PIERROT
She knocked me down!!

(Charlotte sees Don Juan approaching.)

CHARLOTTE
Hey Pierrot, is that the Monsieur?

PIERROT
Uh-huh, that's him.

CHARLOTTE
Oh dear God, how pretty he is, it would have been a pity if he'd of drowned.

PIERROT
I'm going for a drink now. To reset my bones after the beating I've just taken. I'll see you at the church.

(As Pierrot leaves, Don Juan enters with Sganarelle in tow. Charlotte stands aside unseen.)

SCENE 2

DON JUAN

We have missed the mark, Sganarelle. The wind over-
turned both boat and plan, but to tell you the truth our
hostess back there more than made up for the inconvenience. What was her name?

SGANARELLE

Mathurine.

DON JUAN

Mathurine, ah yes, well I find that her charms have quite
expunged my annoyance, and I shan't let her elude me,
even if my pretty peasant girl continues to—indeed I've
arranged things with her so that no matter what happens
I won't be sighing for long.

SGANARELLE

Monsieur, I have to admit you astound me. We've
barely escaped certain death, and instead of giving thanks to God for the mercy he has generously
deigned to show us, you're already busy arousing His
anger again with your endless machinations, and your
freakish, perver—

DON JUAN

Enough!

SGANARELLE

(Addressing himself) Enough, enough, you ignorant
scamp, you know not what you say, let's go!

(Don Juan has seen Charlotte.)

DON JUAN

Aha! *(Aside to Sganarelle)* It is my pretty peasant girl!
(Aloud) Where did this meadow flower pop up from so sud-

denly? Sganarelle, have you ever seen anything so pretty?

SGANARELLE
Never, Monsieur. *(Aside)* Poor piece of goods that she is.

DON JUAN
(To Charlotte) Why, my beauty, this happy meeting? What—in this coastal setting, with only sand and sea and stones about—one finds creatures so exquisite?

CHARLOTTE
Whatever you say, Monsieur.

DON JUAN
Are you from this village?

CHARLOTTE
Yes, Monsieur.

DON JUAN
And you *stay* in it?

CHARLOTTE
Yes, Monsieur.

DON JUAN
And your name is?

CHARLOTTE
Charlotte, here to serve you Monsieur.

DON JUAN
Ah, *what* an enchanting person! And how penetrating her eyes!

CHARLOTTE
Monsieur, you make me all ashamed.

DON JUAN

Oh you mustn't be ashamed if I say what's true. Sganarelle, don't you agree with me? Is she not enchanting?

SGANARELLE

Enchanting, yes.

DON JUAN

(To Charlotte) Turn around for me, if you'd be so kind.

(Charlotte turns in place.)

Oh but your figure is fine! And may I ask you to raise your head?

(Charlotte raises her head.)

Oh but your face has such delicacy! Now let me see your eyes.

(Charlotte looks him in the eye.)

Oh but they're *beautiful*! And your teeth?

(Charlotte smiles at this.)

You smiled! You must be enjoying yourself. Oh, one could love you just for these lovable teeth. Or these appetizing lips. I am undone. I have never met such an attractive person.

CHARLOTTE

Monsieur, it pleases you to say so, but I think maybe you are making fun of me.

DON JUAN

As God is my witness, I already feel too much affection for you to do that. I am speaking from my heart.

CHARLOTTE
I am very much obliged to you if that is true.

DON JUAN
You are not at all obliged to me for *anything* I say, you may thank your own beauty for my compliments.

CHARLOTTE
Monsieur, that's all put too nicely for me, and I don't have the learning to answer you.

DON JUAN
Sganarelle, have a look at her hands!

CHARLOTTE
(Pulling her hands away) No Monsieur, they are filthy as all get-out.

DON JUAN
What are you saying? They are the loveliest hands in the world. Allow me to kiss them, I implore you.

CHARLOTTE
Monsieur, it's too kind what you say. If I'd known you would kiss my hands, I would have rubbed bran on them to clean them.

DON JUAN
And tell me Charlotte, you're not married, are you?

CHARLOTTE
No Monsieur, but I will be soon, to Pierrot, the son of my aunt Simonetta. Who owns a butter churn!

DON JUAN
What? A person of your quality the wife of a simple peasant? No no, it would go against everything you are. You weren't born to stay in the village and make cheese, you

definitely deserve a better future. I see now that Heaven knew this all along and sent me here expressly to prevent this marriage and do proper justice to your charms. Because when all is said and done, beauteous Charlotte, I have come to love you with all my heart, and at a mere word from you I would take you away from this dreadful place and set you up in circumstances befitting your true splendor. My love is very sudden, I know, but what do you expect? It's a flash, a burst, a shiver—sparked by your beauty and nobility. By God, one loves you as much in a quarter of an hour as it would take one six months to love another, less exceptional woman.

CHARLOTTE

Oh really Monsieur, I don't know how you do it when you talk, but what you say makes me feel good, and I want to believe you more than anything. But they always tell me we shouldn't ever believe what noblemen say, and that you courtiers are seducers who are only thinking of leading us common girls astray.

DON JUAN

I'm not one of those people.

CHARLOTTE

Look Monsieur, there is no advantage in letting oneself be led astray. I am a poor peasant girl, but I do have my honor, and I'd rather see myself dead than dishonored. I'd be ruined. I'd lose what little chance I have.

DON JUAN

But how could anyone have the heart to take anything from you? How could anyone be so malicious as to lead you astray? How could *I* be so mean-spirited, so *evil* as to want to dishonor a person like you? No Charlotte, I have a conscience, I couldn't do these things. I love you with every good intention, in the best of faith, and to prove this I must tell you that I fully intend to marry you if you will have me. Do you need further proof? I stand here, ready when you wish, and I call this man as witness to the promise I make you herewith.

(He reaches for her hand, Charlotte pulls it away.)

SGANARELLE
(To Charlotte) Don't be afraid, he'll marry you as many times as you like.

DON JUAN
Oh Charlotte, I realize that you don't know me yet, but you do me an injustice to measure me by other men. There are deceivers at court, you are right...

SGANARELLE
(Cautionary) Monsieur...

DON JUAN
...but you must neither count me as one of them nor doubt the sincerity of my faith. Your beauty and candor should fill you with confidence, for when one is blessed as you are with perfections inside and out, surely one is impervious to old wives' tales. You are not the sort of girl a man could think of leading astray, believe me—you are not a peasant, you are not common, you are more precious than the King is kind.

SGANARELLE
(Aside) Long live the King.

DON JUAN
I'd pierce my own heart with a thousand thrusts of my sword if I thought for an instant of betraying you.

CHARLOTTE
I don't know if what you say is true or not, but you make me believe you.

DON JUAN

You do me justice by believing me—more, you do me honor. And I reiterate my promise with a formal proposal: will you consent, my love, to be my wife?

(A beat.)

CHARLOTTE

As long as my aunt says yes.

DON JUAN

But say, Charlotte, that you wish it for your own part. Give me your hand on it.

(She offers her hand but pulls it back part way.)

CHARLOTTE

But don't go and trick me Monsieur, I beg you. You can see I'm acting in good faith, and it would be on your conscience.

DON JUAN

Alas, still you doubt my sincerity! Shall I swear some frightful oath? "May the souls of murdered men rise up if—"

CHARLOTTE

(Interrupts) Good heavens no! Don't swear that, I believe you.

DON JUAN

Then give me your hand.

CHARLOTTE

(Still hesitant) Monsieur, I…

DON JUAN

Ah, perhaps you will deceive *me*! You are so beautiful,

you won't abandon me for a prince more deserving of your charms?

CHARLOTTE

Oh Monsieur, I could never manage that.

DON JUAN

Then give me a little kiss as a promise.

CHARLOTTE

Oh Monsieur, we have to get married first, please. After that I'll kiss you as much as you like.

DON JUAN

Very well, my beautiful Charlotte, as you wish. Surrender only your hand…

CHARLOTTE

But Monsieur—

DON JUAN

(Interrupts, kneeling before her, kissing her hand) …and suffer me to give voice, through these hundred kisses, to my ravishment and devotion.

(A beat. Charlotte is terribly torn.)

CHARLOTTE

Ah…

DON JUAN

I shall die here before you…

CHARLOTTE

(Sighing) Ah, Monsieur…

(Don Juan pulls her down to the ground. Enter Pierrot.)

SCENE 3

PIERROT
Hold on there Monsieur, step back if you please, you're getting a little too hot, you might give her a fever.

DON JUAN
Who sent *this* whippersnapper?

PIERROT
I'm telling you to step back, you shouldn't be touching my bride.

DON JUAN
(Pushing Pierrot) What a noisemaker.

PIERROT
God be damned but you have no right to push honest people.

CHARLOTTE
Well let him alone yourself, Pierrot.

PIERROT
What? Let him alone? What if I don't want to?

DON JUAN
(Pushing Pierrot harder, cautioning him) Uh uh uh.

PIERROT
God's head, just 'cause you're a big Monsieur you think you can come fondle our women right in front of us. Go fondle your own kind!

DON JUAN
(Knocking Pierrot down) Watch it, boy.

PIERROT

Watch it yourself, God damn it!

(Don Juan kicks Pierrot.)

Don't you kick me!

(Don Juan kicks him again.)

Ah, God be damned!

(Don Juan hits Pierrot.)

God's gut!

(Don Juan hits him again.)

God's blood!

(Don Juan hits him a third time.)

God's *death*!

DON JUAN

You shouldn't take the Lord's name in vain!

SGANARELLE

(Aside) Oh God...

PIERROT

You shouldn't go beating people up! Especially people who saved you from drowning in your big fat clothes!

CHARLOTTE

Pierrot, don't be angry!

PIERROT

I want to be angry, and you're a disgrace, you are, to let him fondle you.

CHARLOTTE

But Pierrot, it's not what you think, Monsieur isn't having his way with me, he's going to *marry* me.

PIERROT

What?! God be damned, you promised to marry *me*!

CHARLOTTE

But that doesn't matter any more Pierrot, 'cause now I can marry a lord, and if you love me you should be glad I have the chance.

PIERROT

Well Hell and Damnation I am *not*—I'd rather see you dead than married to another man!

CHARLOTTE

Come on Pierrot, don't do this. If I'm a lady you'll get something out of it, I'll see to it—you can bring us butter and cheese!

PIERROT

I'll never bring you a thing, even if you pay me double for it! God's gut, if I'd known you'd do this, I would have just smacked him on the head with an oar!

DON JUAN

(Drawing his sword) Watch what you say!

PIERROT

Damn you straight to Hell!

(Don Juan lunges at Pierrot, who jumps behind Sganarelle.)

I'm not afraid of anyone!

(Don Juan stalks Pierrot, who holds Sganarelle between them.)

DON JUAN

Just wait til I get you!

PIERROT

(Moving Sganarelle around as a shield) You make me laugh!

DON JUAN

(Jumping him) Let's see how hard!

PIERROT

(Holding Sganarelle's arms up at Don Juan) I've fought worse than you!

DON JUAN

Ooooo!

SGANARELLE

Leave him alone, Monsieur, the poor wretch, you don't want his blood on your hands. *(To Pierrot)* Listen, go away and don't say anything more to him.

PIERROT

Well I have a lot more to say!

DON JUAN

(Taking a swipe at Pierrot with his sword) I'll teach you how to talk to a gentleman!

PIERROT

(Ducking) No!

(Don Juan cuts Sganarelle's arm instead of Pierrot's.)

SGANARELLE

(Struck) Ah! *(To Pierrot)* The plague on you, you stupid farm boy!

DON JUAN

(To Sganarelle) That's what you get for interfering!

PIERROT

(To Charlotte) He's going to Hell, and you're going with him!

CHARLOTTE

Pierrot!

PIERROT

I'm going to tell your aunt how well you keep house.

(Pierrot storms away.)

DON JUAN

Where were we, ah yes your *hand*—for I am soon to be the luckiest man alive, and I wouldn't trade this happiness for anything in the world! *(Kneeling before her)* What joy, what *rapture* when you are mine and I can—

MATHURINE

(From offstage) Monsieur!

SGANARELLE

Uh-oh, Mathurine.

(Enter Mathurine.)

SCENE 4

MATHURINE

Monsieur.

DON JUAN

(To Charlotte) A moment.

(He leans to Mathurine standing between the two women.)

MATHURINE

Are you making love to Charlotte, Monsieur? Are you talking marriage to her too?

DON JUAN

(Aside to Mathurine) No, on the contrary, it is *she* who was talking marriage to *me*, and I've been trying to tell her I'm engaged to you.

CHARLOTTE

What do *you* want, Mathurine?

DON JUAN

(Aside to Charlotte) She's jealous seeing us together, she wants to marry me...

MATHURINE

I beg your pardon, Charlotte?

DON JUAN

(Aside to Charlotte) ...but I've just told her it's you I want.

MATHURINE

(To Charlotte) Did you address me?

DON JUAN

(Aside to Mathurine) It's useless talking to her...

CHARLOTTE

(To Mathurine) I said "What do you want, Mathurine?"

DON JUAN
(Aside to Mathurine) ...it's fixed in her mind.

CHARLOTTE
(To Mathurine) Well speak up.

DON JUAN
(Aside to Charlotte) Don't even try, she's obsessed with the idea.

MATHURINE
(To Charlotte) I don't think you realize—

DON JUAN
(Aside to Mathurine, interrupting) There's no way to make her listen to reason.

CHARLOTTE
(To Mathurine) You don't think I realize what?

DON JUAN
(Aside to Charlotte) She's obstinate as twenty devils.

(Rapid iambic movement begins here.)

MATHURINE
(To Charlotte) Well I don't think—

DON JUAN
(Aside to Mathurine, interrupting) Avoid her, she's demented.

CHARLOTTE
(To Mathurine) I don't think you—

DON JUAN
(Aside to Charlotte, interrupting) Look at her, she's crazy.

MATHURINE

No, I want to speak with her!

CHARLOTTE

I want to hear her crazy tale!

MATHURINE

You do?

DON JUAN

(Aside to Charlotte) I'll bet she says I asked her for her hand.

CHARLOTTE

Monsieur, you know, has asked—

DON JUAN

(Aside to Mathurine, interrupting) I'll bet she says I promised her my hand.

MATHURINE

(Interrupts, shutting down the iambic movement.) Hold on Charlotte! It's wrong to poach on other people's property.

CHARLOTTE

It's wrong to be jealous if a gentleman prefers to speak to *me*.

MATHURINE

He saw me first.

CHARLOTTE

He saw you first, he saw me second, and the choice was clear. He promised me his hand! *(Pointing to the audience)* Ask them!

MATHURINE
(To Charlotte) Oh Madame, I kiss your hem. Now kiss mine, 'cause it's me he's marrying, not you!

CHARLOTTE
(To Mathurine) Right, and then the *King* will marry you too!

SGANARELLE
(Aside to the audience.) Long live the King.

MATHURINE
Don't mock your betters.

CHARLOTTE
I'm the one.

MATHURINE
You're not!

CHARLOTTE
You'll see.

MATHURINE
It's *me*!

CHARLOTTE
It's *me*!

MATHURINE
Ask him then, he'll tell you if I'm lying.

CHARLOTTE
Is it her, Monsieur, that you promised to marry?

DON JUAN
(Aside to Charlotte) Surely you jest!

MATHURINE
Is it true, Monsieur, you promised her your hand?

DON JUAN
(Aside to Mathurine) What do you *take* me for?

CHARLOTTE
(To Don Juan) But she really believes it!

DON JUAN
(Aside to Charlotte) Let her dream.

MATHURINE
(To Don Juan) Don't you see how she insists it's true?

DON JUAN
(Aside to Mathurine) Let her bark.

CHARLOTTE
(To Don Juan) I want to know the truth.

MATHURINE
(To Don Juan) Enough is enough.

CHARLOTTE
(To Mathurine) I want him to show you up.

MATHURINE
(To Charlotte) I want him to put you down. Like a dog.

CHARLOTTE
Monsieur!

MATHURINE
(To Don Juan) Put her out of her misery.

DON JUAN

(Feigning anger) What can I possibly say?! Each of you maintains that I asked her to be my wife. Now don't you both know what was actually said and where things truly stand without my having to explain further? Must I repeat myself endlessly? The one to whom I gave my promise should happily scoff at the claims of the other. Why should she be at all concerned, if I keep that promise? What lady would question the word of a gentleman?! This bickering profits no one, one must act, not discuss—actions are decisive, all these words merely mask the truth! Only when I marry will this be settled. Only when I marry will you know for sure which of you owns my heart. *(Aside to Mathurine)* Let her think it's hers... *(Aside to Charlotte)* I saw you second... *(Aside to Mathurine)* ...and know that I'm yours. *(Aside to Charlotte)* ...but I place you first. *(Aloud)* I am going now to fetch the priest. I'll be back to find you shortly.

(Exit Don Juan.)

CHARLOTTE

I'm the one he loves.

MATHURINE

I'm the one he'll marry!

SGANARELLE

Stop it! Oh you poor girls, I am sorry for you. I pity your impressionable hearts, and I can't stand here and watch you two race each other off a cliff! Believe me, both of you, don't listen to a word he says, and stay where God put you!

(Don Juan reappears, unobserved.)

DON JUAN

(Aside) Where is Sganarelle, why isn't he—

(He sees Sganarelle.)

SGANARELLE
(Overlapping) My master is a swindler, he plans to deceive you both, as he has deceived so many others before you. He has married the entire human race. What I am trying to say to you is...

(He sees Don Juan listening.)

...totally untrue! And if anyone ever tells you that, you tell him it's all lies. My master is *not* a swindler, he has no plans at present to deceive you, he has never to my knowledge been married to the entire human race, and ah, well, here he is, so you can just ask *him*!

DON JUAN
About what?

SGANARELLE
Monsieur. The world is full of slander and prevarication, and it's best to stay ahead of things, so I was telling them that—

DON JUAN
(Interrupts) Sganarelle.

SGANARELLE
Yes, Monsieur is a respectable and virtuous man. As principled...

CHARLOTTE
(To Don Juan) Monsieur...

SGANARELLE
...and trustworthy...

MATHURINE
(To Don Juan) The priest…

SGANARELLE
…as the King!

SCENE 5

LA RAMÉE
(Entering) Long live the King!

DON JUAN
La Ramée!

LA RAMÉE
(Drawing Don Juan aside) Monsieur, I've come to warn you that you're not safe here.

SGANARELLE
(Aside) I'll say.

DON JUAN
(To La Ramée) Explain!

LA RAMÉE
There are twelve men headed here on horseback. They are closing in on you and should be here any minute. They questioned a young peasant who gave a lengthy description of your clothes. The sooner you escape the better.

DON JUAN
Who are they?

LA RAMÉE
I don't know.

SGANARELLE
(Aside) Probably just old friends.

DON JUAN
(To Charlotte and Mathurine) A pressing matter compels me to leave you now, but I beg you keep in mind my promise and pray for my well-being. You shall have word of me tomorrow.

(La Ramée escorts the ladies away.)

We are outnumbered, we must find a way, a stratagem, to elude our pursuers—Sganarelle!

SGANARELLE
What?

DON JUAN
(Starting to undress) Give me your clothes, and you take mine.

SGANARELLE
(Interrupts) Monsieur, you must be joking, I'll be killed in your clothes.

DON JUAN
(Starting to undress Sganarelle) It's a lucky valet who can have the glory of dying for his master. Hurry up.

SGANARELLE
(Undressing) What an honor.

DON JUAN
Quick.

SGANARELLE
You're welcome.

DON JUAN
(Putting on Sganarelle's jacket) I'll have to have this tailored.

SGANARELLE
You should pay me now.

DON JUAN
You should *obey* me now.

SGANARELLE
(Falling to his knees) Oh God, if I must die, let me die someone else's death and not his!

DON JUAN
Whose death would you rather die than mine? It's bound to be spectacular.

SGANARELLE
(A cry of anguish) No!

DON JUAN
Well find someone else's clothes then, it's your loss.

SGANARELLE
Oh master thank you, you are kind, I'd do anything for you! *(Aside)* One more day of this, then I'm quitting.

(They continue to fumble with the clothes. Transformation to Act III.)

"It's yours if you blaspheme."
Don Juan and the Pauper (III,2), the famous censored scene
Stein, Curtis, McCarter Theatre 2002

"Move away, brother!" Alonso questions his brother's honor (III.4)
Francesca Faridany, Bruce Turk, McCarter Theatre 2002

"Long live the King!"
Sganarelle, sardonic witness to Charlotte's seduction (II,2)
Folmar, McCarter Theatre 2002

"Long live the King!" Members of the company watch the Prologue from the wings
Laura Kenny, Mary Bacon, Ahren Potratz, Steve Hamm, Burton Curtis, McCarter Theatre 2002
All photos: SET Kevin Rupnik, COSTUMES Anna Oliver, LIGHTING Amy Appleyard

"I'll be the avenging angel of Heaven's self-interest."
Don Juan finds a new credo (V,2)
Folmar, Stein, McCarter Theatre 2002

"I shall never repent!" Don Juan rejects the Statue's demand (V,4)
Folmar, Curtis, Cruz, Stein. McCarter Theatre 2002

"Do you mean to beguile us with beautiful words?"
Carlos, as Don Juan renounces Elvira for godly celibacy (V.3)
Folmar, Curtis, Bacon, Turk, Stein, McCarter Theatre 2002

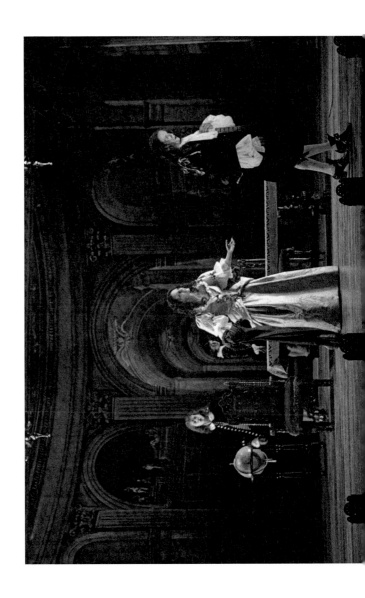

Don Luis leaves his son for the last time,
convinced that Don Juan has found God (V, 1)
Folmar, Frank Corrado, Stein, McCarter Theatre 2002

"I'd never have put good money on this happening." (III,5)
Sganarelle after the Statue nods:
Stein, Folmar, McCarter Theatre 2002

The Statue accepts Don Juan's invitation to dinner (III,5)
Stein, Gilbert Cruz, McCarter Theatre 2002

SCENE 1

(Don Juan and Sganarelle are walking in a for-
est. Don Juan is dressed as his own servant,
Sganarelle as a doctor.)

DON JUAN

I am so happy to be free of all those pesky people.

SGANARELLE

We got out of there just in time, Monsieur, and you have
to admit I was right, these disguises are fantastic, we
blend right in. And I think we're both safer this way.

DON JUAN

Well I'll admit that you look really remarkable. Where
did you scare up that ridiculous outfit?

SGANARELLE

I found it in a pawnshop, and it cost me a pretty penny,
too, but it was worth it. It belonged to a famous doctor,
and the minute I put it on my fortunes changed. People
hold me in higher esteem, they bow to me and even
consult me as a highly qualified professional.

DON JUAN

Consult you how?

SGANARELLE

Well so far six country people, seeing me pass, have
asked my advice about various diseases.

DON JUAN

Which you said you'd never heard of.

SGANARELLE

Nothing doing, not me! I felt obliged to uphold the honor of my apparel and the reputation of its previous owner, so I held forth at length on each ailment, and wrote out prescriptions where appropriate.

DON JUAN

And what remedies did you prescribe for them?

SGANARELLE

Heavens Monsieur, I was grasping at straws, I just wrote whatever came into my head. It would be pretty funny if they all recovered and came flocking to pay me.

DON JUAN

Why shouldn't they? Why shouldn't you claim the privileges enjoyed by all the other quacks, they can't heal people any better than you. All they really do is take the credit when someone doesn't die.

SGANARELLE

So you don't believe in medicine either?

DON JUAN

It is one of mankind's greatest delusions.

SGANARELLE

What? You don't believe in the purgative powers of the senna leaf? In the laxative effects of the cassia fruit? Or in emetic wines that flush the ill humors out of both ends at once?!

DON JUAN

Why do you want me to believe in them?

SGANARELLE

It's all very well for the skeptics to argue against emetic wines, but the Faculty of Medicine will sanction them and win this whole argument.

DON JUAN

If the Faculty of Medicine and its well-placed members sanction emetic wines, it won't be because emetic wines have medicinal value, I assure you. It will be because the Faculty of Medicine stands to benefit from the sale of emetic wines.

SGANARELLE

You really have an evil mind. Emetic wines have been around since long before the current debate—and creating quite a stir whenever they are ingested! There have been miracle results that have converted even the most skeptical minds. Not three weeks ago I—I who speak to you in the third scene of this very play—I witnessed a medical breakthrough.

DON JUAN

And what was that?

SGANARELLE

There was a man who had been in agony for six days. They had tried many remedies but nothing worked, and now they were at a loss. Well at the last minute they thought of emetic wine.

DON JUAN

And so they gave it to him?

SGANARELLE

They winched open his jaw, stuck a tin pump down his throat, and forced this greasy brown liquid through a rusty funnel.

DON JUAN

And he recovered.

SGANARELLE

No, he died.

DON JUAN
Which proves the medicinal value of emetic wine.

SGANARELLE
Oh, it does! The poor man had been trying to die for six days, and that was the only thing that helped him. But let's leave medicine alone, since you have no time for it, and talk of other things. This costume makes me feel quite intellectual, and I'm in the mood to argue a point with you.

DON JUAN
Sganarelle…

SGANARELLE
(Interrupts) You have encouraged me to debate you.

DON JUAN
As long as—

SGANARELLE
(Interrupts) As long as I refrain from finger-wagging…

DON JUAN
Moralizing.

SGANARELLE
…and proselytizing.

DON JUAN
Yes.

SGANARELLE
Well I want to know a little more about how you really think. Is it possible, for example, that you don't believe in God at *all*?

DON JUAN
Wrong topic.

SGANARELLE
That would be a no. And Hell?

DON JUAN
You're moralizing.

SGANARELLE
Another no. Another topic, let's see. Do you believe in the Devil?

DON JUAN
Blah blah blah.

SGANARELLE
Oh, as little as that? How about the afterlife?

DON JUAN
(Cautioning) Sganarelle.

SGANARELLE
(Aside) I can tell he's just yearning to be converted. *(To Don Juan)* All right, how about the Bogeyman? How about the anxious, vengeful ghosts of murdered viceroys—do you believe in them?

DON JUAN
A pox on you.

SGANARELLE
But come on, one has to believe in *something* in this world, so what is it you believe in?

DON JUAN
(Pondering) What is it I believe in?

SGANARELLE

Yes.

DON JUAN

I believe…

(A beat.)

…that two and two are four. And four and four are eight.

SGANARELLE

Well now *there's* a belief system for you! So your religion is arithmetic. Let me see, two hundred women in Gascony plus two hundred women in Aragon equals four hundred women. Amen!

DON JUAN

(Points skyward.) Wasn't it your friend who said, "Be fruitful, and multiply?"

SGANARELLE

What I mean though, Monsieur, is that men can get some pretty misguided notions in their heads, and the more they study, the more stubborn they become. Now I haven't studied as you have, thank God, and no one can boast of ever having taught me a thing, but even with my uncrowded brain and my modicum of judgment I see things more clearly than all your books, and I know perfectly well that this world we are looking at is not a mushroom that just appeared overnight. So I have to ask you—who made these trees, these rocks, this earth, and this sky stretching all around us? Did they make themselves? Did they have parents? And you—standing right there, you for example. Did *you* just happen all by yourself? Didn't your father have to get your mother pregnant to make you? "Exactly," you'll say. "*They* made me, not some holy ghost." Oh but can you think about all these clever inventions that make up the machinery of a man without wondering how it was all fitted together—these nerves, these bones, these veins, these arteries? You don't believe in medicine, so it *must* be God that made them, right? I mean—a lung, think of it! A liver, a heart, a *mind*?! And all the other stuff in there—the *bowels? Oh God interrupt me please,* how can we have a debate if you make no rebuttal and just let me go on babbling out of sheer malice!

DON JUAN
I was waiting for the opening argument to end.

SGANARELLE
My opening argument is that there is something wondrous in mankind, whatever you may say, which all the learned men won't ever be able to explain. I mean, isn't it marvelous that I am standing here, and that I have something in my head that can think a hundred different things in a single minute and can make my body do whatever it wants? Clap my hands, raise my arms, lift my eyes up to Heaven, cry out "*Thank you God!*," shuffle my feet, turn to the right, turn to the left, forward, back, spin around…

(He gets dizzy and falls down.)

DON JUAN
Your argument just doesn't stand up.

SGANARELLE
Oh the Devil! I am so stupid to argue with you. Believe whatever you want, but it really does matter to me that you are going to Hell. You are a lost soul.

DON JUAN
Here we are in agreement. *(Looking around)* Even considering the situation from a purely rational point of

view, it's clear that we are *both* lost. Call that man over
and ask him the way to town.

(A Pauper has appeared.)

SCENE 2

SGANARELLE
(To the Pauper) Comrade, a quick word if you don't
mind. Which way to the village?

PAUPER
Follow this path, Messieurs, and turn right when you
come to the edge of the wood. But be on your guard,
there are thieves about.

DON JUAN
We are obliged to you, my friend, how can we thank
you?

PAUPER
Would you consider helping me with alms, Monsieur?

DON JUAN
Aha! Your kindness comes at a price, I see.

PAUPER
I am a poor man, Monsieur, for many years an almsman
in this wood. I shall certainly pray to God that He give
you everything you desire.

DON JUAN
Be careful what you pray for. If I were you, I'd ask Him
for some decent clothes and stop meddling in other
people's affairs.

SGANARELLE

(To the Pauper) My good man, you don't know Monsieur, he believes only in multiplication.

DON JUAN

What exactly is it you do out here in the forest dark?

PAUPER

All day I pray to God for the health and well-being of the good people who help me.

DON JUAN

You pray for the people who give you something?

PAUPER

With all my heart.

DON JUAN

Well then you must be doing very well for yourself.

PAUPER

Alas Monsieur, I live in the most dire need.

DON JUAN

Surely you jest, a man who prays to God all day for people who give him money must have a thriving business: loads of willing customers, guaranteed results, and to be paid up front and work whenever you want—Sganarelle, think of it!

PAUPER

I assure you, Monsieur, that I often don't have even a crust of bread to eat.

DON JUAN

Well now isn't *that* odd—lots of prayer, nothing to show for it. I think you're being had. You'd be better off at court. I have lots of friends there just like you who sit

around waiting for favors and worshipping idols all day,
but they get richer and richer and richer.

SGANARELLE
(To the Pauper, explaining) He means the King is
generous.

PAUPER
Long live the King.

DON JUAN
Well I'll give you a big shiny louis d'or, if you will be
so good as to curse God.

PAUPER
Ah Monsieur, would you want me to commit such a sin?

DON JUAN
It's all you have to do to get some food and clothes and
a roof over your head. You just have to decide.

(Don Juan produces a large gold coin.)

It's yours if you blaspheme. But you must blaspheme.

PAUPER
Monsieur.

DON JUAN
You won't have it unless you do this.

SGANARELLE
(To the Pauper) Go ahead, blaspheme a little, it won't
hurt you just this once.

DON JUAN
Take it, here it is. Take it I tell you, just curse God.

(The Pauper and Don Juan look into each other's eyes.)

PAUPER

No Monsieur. For the love of God, I would rather die of hunger.

DON JUAN

Well for the love of...my fellow man, I'll give it to you anyway.

(He gives the coin to the Pauper. A commotion offstage draws Don Juan's attention.)

But what cowardice is this? One man attacked by three? I must even the match!

(He rushes off, sword drawn. The Pauper gives the louis d'or to Sganarelle and leaves.)

SCENE 3

SGANARELLE

My master is crazy to look for danger when there's already so much of it looking for him.

(Three thieves flee across the stage. Enter Don Carlos slightly wounded in the hand, followed by Don Juan whose arm has been slightly wounded.)

DON CARLOS

(To Don Juan, watching the thieves flee) I am very glad they're gone, but I am even more grateful to you for helping to rout them. My dear fellow, allow me to offer my thanks for your strong arm and your generous deed—here is a token.

(He offers a purse to Don Juan, who takes it.)

DON JUAN
I have done nothing, Monsieur, that you wouldn't have done in my place. Our very honor is at stake in such situations. For these rogues to ambush you was so cowardly that *not* to fight would have been tantamount to fighting *for* them. *(To Sganarelle)* Doctor, my arm.

(Sganarelle examines and bandages Don Juan's arm.)

(To Don Carlos) But how do you happen to be traveling alone?

DON CARLOS
I was accidentally separated from my brother and our retinue, and when I sought to rejoin them I was set upon by those thieves. They killed my horse, and without your valiant assistance they might well have done the same to me.

DON JUAN
Are you going in the direction of the town?

DON CARLOS
Yes.

DON JUAN
Will you join us? *(Taking his arm back from Sganarelle)* Thank you, Doctor.

(He gives Sganarelle the purse Don Carlos gave him.)

DON CARLOS
No, thank you, we won't be going into the town proper. But you sustained that wound on my account, I cannot

allow you to pay the good doctor. Take this, I beg you.

(He gives Don Juan another purse.)

My brother and I, compelled by one of those vexatious and sensitive matters of honor, must stay on the outskirts and wait for our prey. It is distressing that such matters oblige one to sacrifice one's family name, perhaps even one's own life, but honor is a rigorous taskmaster. What irony that honor often compels us to fight our adversaries to the death, but that dueling is now forbidden. Now one *compromises* one's honor by seeking to defend it, one demands satisfaction only to risk enjoying it in exile and disgrace!

DON JUAN
However, if the authorities don't know about the duel—

DON CARLOS
(Interrupts) But who wishes to live outside the law? You may envy the nobleman's circumstances, but it is a sad thing not to be able to have confidence in one's reputation, to know that one's life, one's peace of mind, and one's worldly possessions depend on the caprice of the first ruffian who takes it into his head to insult one. *(To Sganarelle)* Doctor, my hand.

(Sganarelle examines and bandages Don Carlos' hand.)

DON JUAN
But at least those who insult you are forced to run the same risk and suffer the same anxieties—surely that is some compensation.

DON CARLOS
(To Don Juan) You are a very wise manservant.

DON JUAN

I am at your service, Monsieur. Would it be indiscreet of me to ask what offense has been done you?

DON CARLOS

I will tell you plainly that our sister was seduced and abducted from a convent, and that the author of this injury is a certain Don Juan, son of Don Luis de Tenorio. We have been looking for him for several days and picked up his scent this morning, and we have narrowed the field to this wood. But still we cannot find him. *(To Sganarelle)* Thank you, Doctor.

(He gives Sganarelle a purse.)

DON JUAN

Do you know him personally, Monsieur, this Don Juan of whom you speak?

DON CARLOS

I have never seen him, only heard him described by my brother and others. From all accounts he doesn't have much to recommend him. Clearly his days are numbered.

DON JUAN

Go no further Monsieur, please. He is somewhat dear to me, and it would be cowardly to hear ill spoken of him and stand quietly by. I know you understand these fine points of honor.

DON CARLOS

Of course, dear fellow, I will say nothing more about him. It is the very least I can do for you—you saved my life and inspired my admiration and affection. Nevertheless, whatever friendship you may have for him, I hope you will not find it strange that we seek to redress his wrong.

DON JUAN

On the contrary. I would like to serve you in your quest and spare you any further frustration. I shall take it upon myself to ensure that he gives you satisfaction.

DON CARLOS

Alas, what satisfaction could one possibly give for such a contemptible offense!

DON JUAN

Why, any that your honor might require. I'll see to it that he comes to a place of your choosing at a time that suits you.

DON CARLOS

A sweet hope, my good fellow, to our offended hearts, but after what you've done for me it would grieve me sorely if you were in any way drawn into the affair or put at risk.

DON JUAN

I will be frank. I am so…closely attached to Don Juan that he would not be able to fight without my fighting as well. Indeed, I answer for him as for myself. You have only to tell me when and where you wish to meet him. Doctor, thank you for your discretion in this matter.

(He gives Sganarelle the second purse Don Carlos gave him.)

DON CARLOS

It is a cruel irony of fate that I should owe you my life only to discover that Don Juan is your good friend. *(To Sganarelle)* Indeed, Doctor, our thanks.

(He gives Sganarelle a purse.)

SCENE 4

DON ALONSO
(From offstage) Water the horses and bring them on...

(Enter Don Alonso.)

...I want to take the next stretch on foot.

DON CARLOS
Brother!

DON ALONSO
(Turning at his brother's voice) Brother!

(He sees Don Juan.)

God above, what am I seeing? You with our mortal
enemy!

DON CARLOS
Our mortal enemy?

DON JUAN
(To Don Carlos) Yes, I myself am Don Juan. I say it
freely, though I am outnumbered.

SGANARELLE
Gentlemen, I'm late for an appointment—

DON ALONSO
Move away, brother!

DON CARLOS
(Interrupts) Brother—

DON ALONSO
(Interrupts, drawing his sword and rushing at Don Juan)

Ah traitor, you die at Don Alonso's hand!

DON CARLOS
(Bars Don Alonso's way) Stop brother, I owe him my life!

DON ALONSO
He owes us his!

DON CARLOS
But without his help I would have been killed by thieves just now!

DON ALONSO
Are you suggesting that this should impede our revenge? If you measure his good deed to you against his offense to our family, any thought of gratitude is absurd. The services we receive from an enemy do not bind us. Honor is infinitely more precious than life, so how can you owe your life to a man who has robbed you of your honor? You owe him nothing.

DON CARLOS
It is true, brother, that a gentleman must place honor above all things, but my gratitude to this man in no way diminishes my resentment over his original offense. He will pay for that soon enough, but first I must give him back what he gave me, I must thank him for my life by allowing him the liberty to enjoy—for a short time—what little remains of his.

DON ALONSO
No! We risk too much in putting off our revenge, the opportunity may not come again—Heaven has offered it to us, and it must be snatched! What honor is there in commemorating one's disgrace with the glorification of one's undoer?

DON CARLOS
What honor is there in commemorating one's miraculous rescue with the execution of one's savior?

DON ALONSO
You listen to me—our honor was mortally wounded, we can give our enemy no quarter, there is no propriety here, no seemly recourse in the wake of his unseemly act. If you cannot lend your arm to his punishment, why then withdraw and leave to mine the pleasure of his dispatch. *(To Sganarelle)* Move away, Doctor!

(Sganarelle steps back as Don Alonso rushes at Don Juan. Don Carlos again steps between Don Juan and Don Alonso.)

DON CARLOS
I implore you, brother—

DON ALONSO
(Interrupts) Nothing you can say will change how I feel, he must die!

(He rushes Don Juan again. Don Carlos pulls his sword on Don Alonso. Sganarelle retreats to the bushes.)

DON CARLOS
I tell you brother, you will not take his life today, and I swear to God that I will defend him to the death, even against my own brother. If you kill him, you will kill me first.

DON ALONSO
You should be seized with rancor, brother, but you are meek!

DON CARLOS
Moderation, brother, in all things! Ours must be a *rational*

course, to a just conclusion. Let us not *avenge* our honor in a blind rage, let us *live* it, by mastering our hearts and acting out of gallantry—a gallantry that is not reckless and uncontrolled but born of *reason*, and purity of intention. Our revenge need not be mitigated by this delay, in fact it will be enriched: if we grant him a reprieve now, the fatal blow, when it is struck, will seem more just in the eyes of the world.

DON ALONSO
Are you *blind*, brother? To risk our honor for this fly-by-night notion of indebtedness? For surely you err in your weakness.

DON CARLOS
Rest assured, brother. I may make a mistake, but I shall definitely make amends—this reprieve, which pays my debt in full, increases my hunger for satisfaction. Don Juan, know that I discharge every responsibility with the same passion and thoroughness, and that I shall be no less zealous and uncompromising in addressing your crime than I have been in addressing your kindness to me.

DON JUAN
Monsieur—

DON CARLOS
(Interrupts) I am not interested in your feelings on the matter. I am giving you the opportunity to weigh your conscience: you know the gravity of your offense. I leave you to determine a suitable course of reparation. There are peaceful ways to satisfy us, and there are violent and bloody ways. Whatever choice you make you have promised that Don Juan will meet us on our terms. Kindly purpose to keep that promise, and remember that from the moment I turn my back on you I shall answer only to the honor of my family.

DON ALONSO
(To Don Juan) You are a doomed man.

DON CARLOS
Come, brother.

(Don Carlos and Don Alonso withdraw.)

SCENE 5

DON JUAN
Sganarelle, where are you?

SGANARELLE
(Emerging from the bushes) Here to serve you, Monsieur.

DON JUAN
So you flee when I am attacked?

SGANARELLE
Oh no, Monsieur, I was right in the bushes the whole time.

DON JUAN
I thought Don Carlos quite the honorable fellow. He treated me well, and I rather regret having to kill him.

SGANARELLE
But he hinted at a peaceful solution, you could just as easily choose that option.

DON JUAN
No. My passion for Donna Elvira has now waned completely, and you know that commitment doesn't suit my temperament.

SGANARELLE

Of course Monsieur, why marry her again? They certainly didn't seem to like it the first time around.

DON JUAN

I demand freedom in matters of love, and I could never reconcile myself to the prolonged incarceration of my heart in the tomb of marriage. I am ineluctably, inescapably drawn to what attracts me.

(A tomb comes into view.)

SGANARELLE

Including that?

DON JUAN

But what have we here?

SGANARELLE

You don't know?

DON JUAN

I don't know.

SGANARELLE

It's the tomb the Viceroy was having built when you killed him.

DON JUAN

(Delighted) But of course! I didn't realize it was out here. Everyone has told me what a magnificent work of art it is—and the statue inside, too, I long to see it.

SGANARELLE

Keep your distance, Monsieur.

DON JUAN

Why?

SGANARELLE
Well it isn't polite to drop in on people you've killed.

DON JUAN
It's the very least I can do to pay him a courteous visit,
don't you think, after what I did to him? And if he's a
gentleman he should receive me in kind. Come on.

(Don Juan leads Sganarelle into the tomb.)

SGANARELLE
How beautiful it all is! The marble, the columns, the grandeur—so...*beautiful*. What do you think of it, Monsieur?

DON JUAN
I think it is the last word in vanity and self-aggrandizement.
What I find beautiful is that a man who during his life was
happy with a relatively modest dwelling should want such
a lavish one when he's no longer alive to enjoy it.

SGANARELLE
And the statue!

DON JUAN
My my, isn't he handsome all dressed up as a sort of emperor crusading for the cross. You know, it's curious how
human beings want to be remembered as kings. I wonder
if kings want to be remembered as human beings.

SGANARELLE
Look how well done it is, Monsieur, he really looks like
he did when he was alive. The way he levels his gaze
right at us, it would scare me if I were alone. I don't think
he's very happy to see us.

DON JUAN
Nonsense, it would be appalling of him to disdain my
respectful attentions. Ask him if he'd like to come over

for dinner.

SGANARELLE
I don't think he gets hungry any more.

DON JUAN
I said ask him.

SGANARELLE
Are you joking? It would be crazy to go talking to a statue.

DON JUAN
Do as I tell you.

SGANARELLE
Monsieur Viceroy, this is really so stupid it's laughable, but it's my master who's making me do it. *(To Don Juan)* This doesn't feel—

DON JUAN
(Interrupts) Continue!

SGANARELLE
Monsieur Viceroy, my master, Don Juan, asks if you would do him the honor of dining with him.

(The Statue nods its head yes.)

(Quietly) Oh dear God...

DON JUAN
What is it, what's the matter? Tell me.

SGANARELLE
(Nodding his head as the Statue did) The statue...

(Sganarelle cannot speak.)

DON JUAN
Well, what about the statue? Speak, villain!

SGANARELLE
The statue—it...

DON JUAN
The statue what? I'll beat you if you don't speak.

SGANARELLE
The statue nodded to me.

DON JUAN
A pox on you—

SGANARELLE
(Interrupts) It nodded yes, I'm telling you, as clear as day. Ask him yourself if you don't believe me.

DON JUAN
All right then, you coward, I will. *(To the Statue)* Viceroy, will you dine with me tonight at my house?

(The Statue again nods yes. Don Juan stops dead.)

SGANARELLE
I'd never have put good money on *this* happening.

(A beat.)

DON JUAN
Let's go now.

(Don Juan leaves.)

SGANARELLE
Oh you freethinkers who believe only in science and arithmetic—beware!

(Sganarelle rushes away after Don Juan.

Black out.)

END OF PART ONE.

SCENE 1

*(Don Juan and Sganarelle arrive at Don Juan's
house and are met by servants including Ragotin
and La Violette. Don Juan and Sganarelle change
out of their disguises.)*

SGANARELLE

But Monsieur, I am absolutely convinced it was a phantom.

DON JUAN

Well whatever it was, let's leave it at that, it was a bagatelle, a trifle. We were probably deceived by a trick of the light, or a mist. It's a humid night.

SGANARELLE

Ah Monsieur, we shouldn't be trying to discredit what we plainly saw. He nodded, and it was real, as real as anything on God's earth. I shouldn't wonder if Heaven, scandalized by your life, didn't produce this miracle to pull you back from the brink of—

DON JUAN

(Interrupts) Listen, if you pester me any more with your idiotic reflections on morality, if you insist on putting your religious superstitions before simple logic, I'll do to you what the church has so often done to people who put simple logic before religious superstition—I'll call for the lash, have you held down by men in hoods, and whip you until you can't speak. Are you hearing me clearly?

SGANARELLE

Very clearly, Monsieur, clear as a bell, you couldn't be clearer. You know, that's one of your really admirable qualities, you don't beat around the bush, you just say exactly what you think. Oh, you have so *many* admirable qualities—

DON JUAN

(Interrupts) Enough. It's late, I'm hungry, and I want dinner as soon as possible. *(To Ragotin)* A chair, boy.

SCENE 2

LA VIOLETTE

Monsieur, you have a visitor. Your tailor, Monsieur Dimanche, has been waiting some time to see you. He says it is a pressing matter and insists on speaking to you.

SGANARELLE

That's just what we need now, creditors. Honestly, I'd like to know where these working-class people get the nerve to actually ask for their money. Didn't you tell him Monsieur was not at home?

LA VIOLETTE

I have told him that at least once an hour.

SGANARELLE

Well he can wait as long as he wants.

DON JUAN

(To La Violette) No, actually, show him in.

(Exit La Violette.)

It's very bad strategy to hide from creditors. I'll send him away satisfied without giving him a penny, you watch.

(Enter Monsieur Dimanche.)

Scene 3

DON JUAN
Ah, Monsieur Dimanche, come in, come in! I am thrilled
to see you and appalled that the servants didn't show
you in the very instant you arrived. I gave orders that
I would see no one under any circumstances, but that
would never include *you*—good God, what can they
have been thinking? The door is always open to you
chez moi. You are a dear friend, that much at least is
due you.

MONSIEUR DIMANCHE
Monsieur, I am very much obliged—

DON JUAN
(Interrupts) God's gut, you rascals, I'll show you what
happens when you leave Monsieur Dimanche in the
waiting room for— *(To Monsieur Dimanche)* How long
were you out there?

MONSIEUR DIMANCHE
Four hours, Monsieur, but—

DON JUAN
(Interrupts, to the servants) Four hours?! When will
you oaves learn who is who?

MONSIEUR DIMANCHE
Monsieur, it is nothing really.

DON JUAN
(To the servants) You said I wasn't home to Monsieur
Dimanche?! He's my best friend!

MONSIEUR DIMANCHE
Monsieur, I am your *servant.* And I have come—

DON JUAN
(Interrupts, to the servants) Come now, a chair for Monsieur Dimanche.

MONSIEUR DIMANCHE
I am quite comfortable as I am, Monsieur.

DON JUAN
Not at all, not at all, I want you to sit with me, right next to me in fact.

MONSIEUR DIMANCHE
Oh no, Monsieur, I—

DON JUAN
(Interrupts, to the servants) Take away this…*campstool*, and bring a proper chair.

MONSIEUR DIMANCHE
Heavens no, Monsieur, this is not appropriate—

DON JUAN
(Interrupts) Nonsense! I owe you so much, why should you stand while I sit? These social distinctions are odious.

(A proper chair arrives.)

SGANARELLE
(To Monsieur Dimanche) There you go, Monsieur, pray be seated.

DON JUAN
(Interrupts) Sit yourself down with me, I insist!

MONSIEUR DIMANCHE
No Monsieur, I am perfectly all right. I came to—

DON JUAN
(Interrupts) Now my dear Dimanche, I won't hear a
word you say until you are seated.

MONSIEUR DIMANCHE
I'll do as you wish, Monsieur, but—

DON JUAN
(Interrupts) By God, Monsieur Dimanche, you are looking marvelous.

MONSIEUR DIMANCHE
Thank you Monsieur, I am—

DON JUAN
(Interrupts) You are the very picture of health—rosy
cheeks, ruby lips, sparkling eyes!

MONSIEUR DIMANCHE
I would appreciate it, Monsieur, if—

DON JUAN
(Interrupts) And your waistcoat is superb, I want one
just like it.

MONSIEUR DIMANCHE
Monsieur, I—

DON JUAN
(Interrupts) Though just a bit smaller...[7]

MONSIEUR DIMANCHE
I have come about the b—

DON JUAN
(Interrupts) And your wife, Monsieur Dimanche, Madame Dimanche—she is also well?

---

[7] "smaller" is exchangeable for bigger, longer, shorter, or whatever word best de-
scribes the difference in size between the actors playing Don Juan and Dimanche

MONSIEUR DIMANCHE
Very well, Monsieur, God be praised.

DON JUAN
Now there's a handsome woman!

MONSIEUR DIMANCHE
She is at your service, Monsieur.

DON JUAN
Is she now.

MONSIEUR DIMANCHE
The reason I have come—

DON JUAN
(Interrupts) And your little girl Claudine. How is she?

MONSIEUR DIMANCHE
Just as well as she could be.

DON JUAN
She is really coming into her own.

MONSIEUR DIMANCHE
She is also at your service, Monsieur.

DON JUAN
Well I am at hers, pretty girl that she is. I love everything about her.

MONSIEUR DIMANCHE
You do us honor, Monsieur. But Monsieur—

DON JUAN
(Interrupts) And your little son Alphonse, is he still making a racket on that little drum.

MONSIEUR DIMANCHE
He loves his drum, Monsieur.

DON JUAN
How charming—

MONSIEUR DIMANCHE
(Interrupts) He bangs away, night and day.

DON JUAN
Why that's—

MONSIEUR DIMANCHE
(Interrupts) He simply can't be stopped!

DON JUAN
Monsieur, I—

MONSIEUR DIMANCHE
(Interrupts) My wife was really driven mad by it.

DON JUAN
How can I help you today?

MONSIEUR DIMANCHE
(Interrupts) So finally she gave him a good smack and took it away.

DON JUAN
Are you here on business?

MONSIEUR DIMANCHE
(Interrupts) But Alphonse had a fit, you should have seen him.

DON JUAN
Have you come about the bill?

MONSIEUR DIMANCHE
(Interrupts) He screamed and screamed and screamed, so she had to give it back.

(Monsieur Dimanche turns and looks at Don Juan. A beat.)

DON JUAN
Well I'd better not give him a drum next year.

MONSIEUR DIMANCHE
Now Monsieur, I've come about the bill—

DON JUAN
(Interrupts) And your little dog—

SGANARELLE
Brusqué.

DON JUAN
Brusqué! Does he still snarl as loud as ever? And bite the leg of every visitor?

MONSIEUR DIMANCHE
It's actually gotten worse, Monsieur. I'm afraid we'll never be able to bring him to heel.

DON JUAN
Don't be surprised if I ask about everyone in your family—I take a great interest in them all.

MONSIEUR DIMANCHE
We are infinitely grateful, Monsieur, and speaking of interest—

DON JUAN
(Interrupts) Monsieur Dimanche, always be my friend!

MONSIEUR DIMANCHE
Why Monsieur, I insist—

DON JUAN
(Interrupts) Your hand on it!

MONSIEUR DIMANCHE
(Taking Don Juan's hand) I am at your disposal, Monsieur.

DON JUAN
By God I am at yours, and wholeheartedly.

MONSIEUR DIMANCHE
You do me too much credit, Monsieur—

DON JUAN
(Interrupts) There is nothing I wouldn't do for you.

MONSIEUR DIMANCHE
And speaking of credit—

DON JUAN
(Interrupts) But let's not stand on ceremony! Dine with me, Monsieur Dimanche!

MONSIEUR DIMANCHE
I am flattered, Monsieur, but I must be getting home, and before I go—

DON JUAN
(Interrupts, to the servants) Ho there, a torch for Monsieur Dimanche, unfortunately he must be going now. Have four or five of my men escort him home with muskets.

MONSIEUR DIMANCHE
That won't be necessary, I can make my own way home, but it *is* necessary that we—

DON JUAN
(Interrupts) What, no escort? I won't hear of it! I am your servant, and furthermore I am in your debt.

MONSIEUR DIMANCHE
Since you put it that way, Monsieur—

DON JUAN
(Interrupts) You have made all my favorite clothes!

MONSIEUR DIMANCHE
I came about the bill, Monsieur—

DON JUAN
(Interrupts) Shall I take you home myself?

MONSIEUR DIMANCHE
No, Monsieur!!

DON JUAN
I see that I have offended you, Monsieur Dimanche, I am mortified. Dear friend, I know when it's time to leave. I implore you, be assured of my devotion to you and your family. There is nothing I wouldn't do to serve you.

(Don Juan withdraws.)

SGANARELLE
I must say, my master thinks the world of you.

MONSIEUR DIMANCHE
It seems so—he makes so many courtesies and compliments that I never have the chance to ask for my money. But he is such a thoughtful man, I can't go away angry.

SGANARELLE
Actually we all feel the same way about you.

MONSIEUR DIMANCHE

That's nice, you don't all owe me nearly as much.

SGANARELLE

You know, maybe if something happened to you—if somebody beat you really really badly with a truncheon, then maybe you'd understand how strongly we feel about you.

MONSIEUR DIMANCHE

(Interrupts) Sganarelle, I beg you to say a little word to him about the money owing.

SGANARELLE

Listen, I bet if you asked him one more time, he'd give you exactly what's coming to you.

MONSIEUR DIMANCHE

And Sganarelle, *your* bill is rather high.

SGANARELLE

Oh, it's my pleasure, don't mention it.

MONSIEUR DIMANCHE

But I—

SGANARELLE

(Interrupts) The very least I can do for you is give you my business.

(He starts to push Monsieur Dimanche toward the door.)

MONSIEUR DIMANCHE

I want the money I'm owed!

SGANARELLE

We all do, but that doesn't mean he'll give it to us.

MONSIEUR DIMANCHE
He doesn't pay you either?

SGANARELLE
A tip here and there but no wages in ages.

MONSIEUR DIMANCHE
(With a derisive chuckle) Just like a nobleman, ha!

SGANARELLE
(Playing offended) But how can you joke about this?

MONSIEUR DIMANCHE
I fully intend to—

SGANARELLE
(Interrupts) You fully intend to joke about this?

MONSIEUR DIMANCHE
I see what you're up to—

SGANARELLE
(Interrupts) You have insulted me!

MONSIEUR DIMANCHE
You—

SGANARELLE
(Interrupts) I will have satisfaction!

MONSIEUR DIMANCHE
I—

SGANARELLE
If you don't leave the stage right now I'll kill you!

*(He pushes Monsieur Dimanche out the door. Don
Juan reappears. La Violette enters.)*

SCENE 4

LA VIOLETTE
Monsieur, your father is in the foyer.

DON JUAN
Oh *perfect*. One idiot drives me to the brink, and another
delivers the *coup de grâce*.

(Enter Don Luis.)

DON LUIS
(To Don Juan) I see that I have caught you unawares.
You are embarrassed, and wish that I hadn't come. It is
strange how we have come to plague each other so. If
you are disappointed that I keep returning, I am equally
disappointed by the way you live, blind to the decen-
cies that bind all honorable people together. Alas, we
can see and know so little of what we do if we do not
trust God to illumine our paths, if we presume to know
better than He and to goad Him with blind desires and
selfish demands.

I yearned for a son, and with a longing I have never
felt in any other attainment. I prayed for you ceaselessly,
day and night, with all the fervor in my soul. And this
son, for whom I wearied Heaven with vows and offerings
and an ecstasy of prayer, is the sorrow and torment of my
heart—of which I believed he'd be the greatest joy and
consolation. Tell me how to look at the life of that child
now; how to conceive of this multitude of thoughtless,
dishonorable, cruel misdeeds; how to excuse them in the
eyes of a world that turns away appalled. This endless
trail of disgrace has forced me time and again to implore
the indulgence of the King, and I have nearly exhausted
his patience—and in so doing I have called into question
the very value of my own services to the throne and the
credibility of those loyal to me.

DON JUAN
Long live the King.

DON LUIS
How could you have sunk so low? Aren't you ashamed to betray the opportunities of your noble beginnings? Is there some pride you take in defiling them? And have you the right to bring our family down? What have you done in the world that you call yourself a *noble*man? Do you think that it suffices to bear a name and a coat of arms, that being descended from a noble line makes you noble, even if you live outside the law? No, my son, a birthright must be substantiated in living deed by its beneficiary, and there is no chance of doing so where virtue is absent. We have no right to the name and reputation of our ancestors unless we do everything in our power to emulate them. In fact the legacy of their achievements *obliges* us to honor them—to follow in their path and to uphold their standards—if we wish to be their true heirs. But as you dishonor them, they disclaim you. You have made nothing of the light they hold up for you; it serves only to show, to every single person who looks at you, the shame of your life's work.

A nobleman has advantages that must be used for the good of all people, he does not take advantage of all people for his own good. The world looks to him as to a king. Never forget that the nobleman who lives in infamy betrays nature; that goodness is the first qualification of nobility; that the name one signs is far less meaningful than what one does with the gift of life. I would respect the son of a laborer who lives honorably more than the son of a king who lives as you do.

(A beat.)

DON JUAN
Monsieur, if you were seated, you could talk *forever* and not get tired.

DON LUIS

I want neither to sit nor to talk any more. Insolent boy, I can see that your heart is closed to all that I say. But know, my unworthy son, that a father's love is strained to the limit by all the miseries you have wrought. Know that I could let loose the judgment of Heaven and call an end to your licentiousness. Perhaps I could wash away, by your punishment, the shame of having given you life.

(Don Luis leaves.)

SCENE 5

DON JUAN

(Calling after Don Luis) Oh, just *die*, and the sooner the better, it's the best thing you could do. Everyone has to die, and fathers are supposed to die first—it's unbearable when they don't.

SGANARELLE

(Shocked) Ah Monsieur, that's terrible, you're wrong!

DON JUAN

I'm wrong?

SGANARELLE

Yes, it's terrible.

DON JUAN

(Rising in anger) Wrong, did you say?

SGANARELLE

Yes Monsieur, you're wrong! It's terrible... You should have—

DON JUAN

(Interrupts, angry) I should have what?

SGANARELLE

You should have thrown him out, I mean, have you ever seen anything so impertinent? For a father to come protesting his love to his son, telling him to mend his ways, reminding him of his family honor, wishing he'd lead the life of a noble man, suggesting he trust in God, and a hundred other stupid things like that—and you haven't even eaten! How can a man like you endure it? You know how to live, you don't need that! I admire your patience. *(Aside, to himself)* Damn you Sganarelle for playing along! When will you speak your mind?

DON JUAN

Give me supper now, before anyone else arrives.

(Enter Ragotin.)

RAGOTIN

There's a woman outside, Monsieur.

DON JUAN

At this hour? Who could it be?

RAGOTIN

She is veiled, Monsieur, I couldn't tell.

SGANARELLE

(Heading to the door) I'll go see.

(Donna Elvira appears.)

Scene 6

DONNA ELVIRA

You are surprised, Don Juan, to see me at this hour, and still in these clothes. But a pressing matter brings me, and it cannot be left unspoken for a moment longer. I do

not come in anger, as I did this morning. I am changed.
I am no longer the Elvira who spat threats at you and
longed only for vengeance. Heaven has banished those
unworthy passions from my heart—the wild transports
of unrequited love, the shameful obsession with desire,
base and temporal. And what remains in my heart? A
devotion cleansed of every sensual concern, an almost
sacred tenderness, a love not of the flesh but of the
spirit—a love that thinks not of itself but only of your
happiness and peace.

DON JUAN
(To Sganarelle) You're weeping.

SGANARELLE
Yes, forgive me.

DONNA ELVIRA
It is this perfect, pure love that brings me here to your
heart, to open your eyes to Heaven's omens, to reach out
and pull you back from the precipice on which you stand.
Yes, Don Juan, I know what you have done. I know that
I am one of many who have died by your hand or suffered at your caress. The same God whose healing vision
has helped me to see my own errors has led me here to
help you see yours. Your transgressions have exhausted
Heaven's patience, and the full measure of its fury stands
poised to crash down upon you. But by God's grace you
may yet disarm Heaven's rage with repentance, simple
and swift. Perhaps you haven't even a day left to you,
or even what remains of this night, to unlink your fate
from that greatest of all miseries.

I, who bring you this message, release you from
my grasp, from any obligation to me. I am recovered,
by the grace of Heaven, from the madness that seized
and confused my mind. I shall return to the convent and
pray only for time enough, in this life, to atone for the
mistakes I have made and to earn, through an absolute

penitence, forgiveness for the condemnable selfishness of my passion. But I would never be free of grief, even in my retreat, if a person I had loved so dearly and tenderly as you were made an example of Heaven's irrevocable judgment. If I could persuade you to dispel the frightful curse that hangs over you, it would give me joy past believing. I beg you with these tears—do not refuse me your salvation, your penitence, your peace.

SGANARELLE

Poor woman.

(A beat. Don Juan is silent.)

DONNA ELVIRA

I loved you with too much intensity. Nothing in the world had ever seemed so dear to me, everything I did I did thinking of you, I broke my vows for you, I brought shame to my family for you. I am asking you, in return, only that you put a stop to your own undoing and start your life anew. Save yourself, Don Juan, I ask it of you one more time. If the tears of a person you once loved are not enough, I urge you to it by whatever it is that can still touch your heart.

(Don Juan doesn't respond.)

SGANARELLE
(Aside) He has the heart of a tiger!

DONNA ELVIRA

I will leave you now. I have said everything I came to say.

DON JUAN

Madame, it is late. Stay here with us, I will see to your every comfort.

DONNA ELVIRA

No, Don Juan, I am no longer yours to hold back.

(Don Juan steps between her and the door.)

DON JUAN

But Madame, it would give me great pleasure if you stayed, I assure you. It is a dark night, and late.

DONNA ELVIRA

It *is* a dark night...and late—too late to waste time with temptations and trifling remarks. Let me go now, quickly.

(She goes to the door. Don Juan takes a torch and follows her.)

(Turning back) You need not show me out. Think only of my words. May you make use of them. Farewell.

(Donna Elvira leaves.)

SCENE 7

DON JUAN

You know, I really do feel some little something for her, even still? I found a kind of pleasure in seeing this great change in her—her clothes, all untended, her exhaustion, and her tears have stirred in me the half-remembered embers of a fire long extinguished.

SGANARELLE

It was only last week.

DON JUAN

I am tempted to try and break down her resistance one more time.

SGANARELLE

You mean her words had no effect on you?

DON JUAN

On the contrary, they were like an apéritif, they stimu-
lated my appetite. I want my dinner.

SGANARELLE

Very well. But Monsieur, did you not hear what she just
said? Because if she had said that to me, and I were you,
I would be looking at things in a very different light. I
would be thinking about reforming.

DON JUAN

You're right, Sganarelle, I should really think about
reforming, shouldn't I?

SGANARELLE

Indeed you should.

DON JUAN

Yes, by God, I should. Twenty or thirty more years of
this life, and then we'll discuss it.

SGANARELLE

(Shocked) Ah!

DON JUAN

What do you think of that plan?

SGANARELLE

Here's your dinner.

*(He sneaks some food from a plate and eats it.
Don Juan sees him chewing.)*

DON JUAN

You know, I think your cheek is swollen. What's the

matter? Maybe we should call a doctor. *(Looking at the wines)* Burgundy, Chablis, is there no emetic wine in my cellar? *(To the servants)* And the rusty funnel, too, we might have to operate. *(To Sganarelle)* How are you feeling?

SGANARELLE

(Speaking with his mouth full) Perfect, fine.

DON JUAN

What?

SGANARELLE

(Mouth still full) Nothing.

DON JUAN

Let's have a look.

(He grabs Sganarelle.)

God's gut, is it a goiter? Is the devil in you? *(To the servants)* Call a priest, quick—and something to lance it with. *(Seizing a knife from the table)* It's ripe for popping. Hurry, he'll die!

(He holds the knife to Sganarelle's neck.)

Well aren't you a rascal, eating my dinner.

SGANARELLE

Monsieur, I was worried maybe your chef had put in too much salt and pepper.

DON JUAN

I think you're hungry.

SGANARELLE

I *am* hungry.

DON JUAN

Well, sit and eat with me, there's something I want to ask you after dinner.

(Sganarelle sits and eats. The servants swirl about serving and taking away various dishes.)

SGANARELLE

Well this is perfect, Monsieur, I haven't eaten a thing since this morning. Good Lord, taste that, that's really as good as it gets. And what a day—first poor Gusman, then Donna Elvira, and the boat trip, and swimming for our lives... *(To the servants, snapping his fingers)* My plate, my plate! Hey take it easy, if you don't mind. *(To Don Juan)* That peasant boy, the women fighting, the Pauper in the forest...

(Don Juan stands up abruptly.)

Monsieur...

(A beat. Sganarelle looks at Don Juan.)

(Digging in again) That is a roast among roasts. *(To Ragotin)* God's gut, little fellow, how clever you are at handing out clean plates! *(To Don Juan)* And I loved the scene with the two brothers hee-hawing about their honor. During which, as you may recall, I thoroughly evacuated my bowels.

DON JUAN

(Interrupts) I remember.

SGANARELLE

Bon appétit.

DON JUAN

Thank you.

SGANARELLE

You're welcome. How can you eat food and not believe in God?

DON JUAN

I believe in the money that bought it.

SGANARELLE

Speaking of money—

(La Violette leans between Don Juan and Sganarelle to pour the wine.)

SGANARELLE

La Violette, where did you learn to bring the wine at the perfect moment like that? Superb. *(To Don Juan)* How many prescriptions did I write out, and not once in all that time did I have so much as a crust of— *(To the servants)* God be damned, as the peasant boy said—more food! *(To Ragotin)* Tell the chef he didn't make enough. *(To Don Juan)* I understand Epicurus now: he sought pleasure to escape trouble. What is this?

DON JUAN

A parsnip.

SGANARELLE

Oh, I don't like that. *(To a servant)* No, we want the pudding *with* the pork. *(To a servant)* Pudding *now*! *(Slapping a servant's hand)* Leave that there. *(To Don Juan)* Have some lard. *(To a servant)* Get the ham! *(To another servant)* Take my plate! *(To Don Juan)* Pass the lard. And then your father—

(Don Juan stands abruptly, annoyed.)

Oh my dear...

(A beat.)

(Throwing his head back, exclaiming) Chicken pie! *(To Don Juan, winking)* Peasant girl! *(Aside)* Getting paid! *(To a servant)* Trifle now. *(To another servant)* Macaroons. *(To Don Juan)* Macaroons? *(To the servant)* Macaroons. *(To Don Juan)* Pay me soon. *(To a servant)* And bring some spoons. *(To Don Juan)* Armagnac? *(To a servant)* Armagnac. *(To another servant)* Give that back! *(To Don Juan)* Now what did you want to ask me?

(He and Don Juan look at each other. There are three loud knocks at the door. Everyone onstage stops dead.)

DON JUAN
We should at least be allowed to dine in peace.

SGANARELLE
(To the servants) No more guests until we're through.

(Again three loud knocks. Sganarelle gets up.)

Allow me, I'll take care of it myself.

(Sganarelle goes to the door.)

DON JUAN
Who could knock like that?

(Sganarelle returns, frightened.)

SGANARELLE
Monsieur...

DON JUAN
Who is it? What's the matter?

SGANARELLE

The... It's there.

DON JUAN

What?

SGANARELLE

The...

DON JUAN

(To the servants) Answer the door.

(The servants back away. Sganarelle crosses himself.)

You cowardly *idiots*, I'll go myself. I'm damned if a knock on the door is going to start *me* praying.

(Don Juan goes to the door.)

SGANARELLE

Ah, poor Sganarelle, where can you hide?

(Don Juan reenters, followed by the Statue.)

SCENE 8

DON JUAN

(To the servants) Get a chair, and set another place. And quickly, come on, Sganarelle, join us.

SGANARELLE

Monsieur, I'm not hungry any more.

DON JUAN

Nonsense, sit down, I tell you! Let's drink. *(Raising a glass)* To the Viceroy's health, Sganarelle.

SGANARELLE
Monsieur, I'm not thirsty any more.

DON JUAN
(To the servants) A glass for the Viceroy! *(To Sganarelle)* Drink, I tell you! And sing a song to amuse our guest.

SGANARELLE
(Touching his throat) Monsieur, I'm not in good voice.

DON JUAN
That doesn't matter, come on! *(To the servants)* And the rest of you, accompany him. Bring a lute. Ragotin!

THE STATUE
Don Juan.

(Everyone stops still.)

Enough. I have come to invite you to dine with me to-morrow. Have you the courage to accept?

DON JUAN
Yes! I accept. I'll just bring Sganarelle along.

SGANARELLE
Thank you, but tomorrow is my fasting day, I won't be able to join you, sorry.

THE STATUE
(To Don Juan) I will come for you tomorrow evening.

DON JUAN
(Offering a torch to the Statue) A torch to light your way.

THE STATUE
I have no need for a torch. Heaven lights the way.

*(The Statue leaves. Don Juan is transfixed.
Transformation to Act V.)*

ACT FIVE

SCENE 1

*(Don Luis has returned to Don Juan's house to
find his son in an attitude of prayer.)*

DON LUIS
Oh my son, is it possible that kind Heaven has granted
my deepest wish? Is it possible that what I am seeing is
really true? You are not giving me false hope, I can be
sure of this sudden change in you? You have repented?

DON JUAN
Yes. I have acknowledged my mistakes. I have come
back. I am not the man I was last night. Heaven has ef-
fected an astonishing change, it has touched my spirit and
undeceived my eyes, and I look back with horror on the
long dissolution of my life, on its chaos and criminal-
ity. I have mulled over in my mind and heart all these
abominations, and it amazes me that God could have
indulged them for so long without punishing me many
times over with the full force of His justice. Indeed He
hasn't punished me at all, but shown me favor, and I intend to honor His generosity as I ought, to make it clear
to everyone that I have changed, to make amends for past
depravities and misdeeds, and to do everything I can to
deserve Heaven's complete forgiveness. I shall strive
towards these things, and I beg you, Monsieur, to hold
me to my purpose, and to help me to find a person who
can guide me, someone under whose guidance I might

learn to walk safely on the road I now must follow.

DON LUIS

Dear son, how easily a father's tenderness and love are recalled, and how quickly a son's offenses evaporate at the first words of repentance and regret. All the sadness you have caused me is effaced by your resolve. My sorrow is already forgotten, these are tears of joy. All my prayers are answered, and I have nothing more to ask of Heaven. Embrace me, and persist, I urge you, in your commendable purpose. I am with you.

(Don Juan embraces Don Luis.)

Now I must be off to take the happy news to your mother, to share with her my excitement, and my contentment. And to give thanks to God for the pious resolutions He has deigned to inspire in you. Goodbye, my son.

(Don Luis leaves. Stillness.)

SCENE 2

SGANARELLE

Oh Monsieur, how happy I am to see you changed. It's a long time now I have hoped for this, and now look— thanks to Heaven, my wish has come true.

DON JUAN

(Without moving) A pox on you, fool.

SGANARELLE

I know, I am still a fool, but what's important is that *you* are changed.

DON JUAN

I didn't mean you.

SGANARELLE

Ah, yes, well, perhaps you *were* a fool, but not any more.

DON JUAN

What, you think I meant what I said to him? You think my tongue speaks for my heart?

SGANARELLE

I think you meant it, yes, of course you meant it.

DON JUAN

(Interrupts) No! No! I am not in the least changed. My feelings haven't changed, my point of view hasn't changed—none of it!

SGANARELLE

But you do acknowledge the miracle—the statue walking, and talking to you, surely you must give over to this!

DON JUAN

There is certainly something there, and I don't understand it, but whatever it might be, it isn't about to change my mind or soften my will.

SGANARELLE

You were just…you mean you really…but you said—

DON JUAN

(Interrupts) I said I intended to modify my behavior, and to throw myself into living a morally incorruptible life— well, the devil take me if I haven't found a way to do just that. I see it clearly now, it's pure logic—an expedient stratagem whereby I resolve to control myself in order to humor my father, whom frankly I *need*, and then merely switch sides. I'll take the side of all those annoying people who constantly bear down on me with their punitive, moralizing admonitions. I shall become like them, and

behind this mask find freedom at last. Sganarelle, I need to have someone who can see the depths of my soul and understand why I do things the way I do.

SGANARELLE
But Monsieur, still you believe in nothing? And even so intend to pose as a respectable man?

DON JUAN
Why not? There are so many like me who want to have their way with the world and who avail themselves of the same pretense to do so.

SGANARELLE
Ah, what a man! What a man!

DON JUAN
There is no shame in it. These days hypocrisy is the most fashionable vice of all. And all fashionable vices pass as virtues. And the most coveted role in this drama is the part of the respectable man, because it masks the largest number of vices. To unite hypocrisy and respectability is to have wonderful advantages in our society. People have great regard for respectable men and place their trust in them. The deceptions of a respectable man usually go unnoticed, and when they *are* noticed, who dares say anything?

It's perfect—all the other vices are open to censure, anyone on the street is at liberty to condemn them, but hypocrisy is invisible, a uniquely privileged vice that stops all mouths and enjoys an impunity as unquestioned as the King's own.

SGANARELLE
Long live the King!

DON JUAN
One has only to affect piety and join the tightly knit ranks

of like-minded dissemblers. Then if a person should try
to expose one of your number, he arouses the ire of the
whole club, and all of you turn against him—even if you
all know he is acting in good faith and is in fact a genuinely
good man. Of course, a man like that always makes the
best dupe. He falls right into the hypocrites' trap and un-
wittingly *supports* their secret activities, while they make
an intimidating public show of censorious solidarity, and
effectively silence, even ruin, the hapless intruder. Oh,
how many do you suppose I have known who by this very
scheme have dressed up the sins of their youth to look like
something else, who have found a safe haven under the
cloak of piety, who in that subtle disguise have found the
freedom to be the wickedest men of all? How many bakers
and bankers and brokers? How many clerks, clerics, kings?
You might see what they're up to and know them for what
they are, but all they have to do is lower their heads, utter a
humble sigh or two, and roll their eyes heavenwards, and
the world will happily forgive what they've done. And if
they accuse someone else of what they do all the time,
the world, by believing them, gives them license to do it
again and again and again.

This is exactly how I shall now protect my interests,
exempting myself from any further censure and actually *enhancing* my reputation. Everyone will be happy.
I won't give up a single one of my cherished pursuits,
but I'll take care to indulge myself covertly and with a
minimum of noise, and if anyone finds me out I'll call
on my cabal, unworried and unhurried, and those terribly
pious friends will immediately close ranks and vindicate
my name. I'll never forgive the man who questions my
conduct—I'll patiently nurse an irreversible grudge. I'll
set myself up as the censor of other people's actions—of
social mores, of religious observance, of scientific papers,
of the press, of pamphlets and theatrical entertainments.
I'll report on my findings to the appropriate authorities,
whom I shall befriend, then replace, then destroy. I'll
find everyone wanting, and have a high opinion only

of myself. I'll be the avenging angel of Heaven's self-interest and keep my enemies ever further at bay. I'll accuse them of godless secrets and unleash against them the religious extremists who, ignorant of the reason and confident of my friendship, will overwhelm them with slander and abuse, denouncing them loudly on their own personal God-given authority, then hound them off the public stage forever. I shall seem altruistic and be ruthless, I shall use every ruse of church and state and finance to become untouchable, I shall exploit the fallibilities of every man I meet. For this is the way a sensible man profits from the weaknesses of men and capitalizes on the vices of his age!

SGANARELLE

God in Heaven, what am I hearing? All you needed was to become a hypocrite to achieve the pinnacle of wickedness! You were always a bad man, but you were always true to yourself. Monsieur, this last speech of yours appalls me, I can no longer prevent myself from speaking my mind. Do what you will with me—whip me, beat me to a pulp, kill me if you want, but I must unburden my heart. And remember that I speak as a *faithful* valet, and faithful I shall remain until you pay me my last wage. Oh, I must summon all my wits and talk pure logic so that you cannot dismiss what I say!

You must know, Monsieur, that a pitcher goes only so many times to the well before it finally cracks. Look, as that writer said, whose name I can't recall at the moment—a man is, in this world, like a bird on a branch. The branch clings to the tree. He who clings to the tree follows sensible rules, sensible rules are worth more than clever speeches, clever speeches are found at court, *courtiers* are found at court, courtiers follow trends, trends are figments of the imagination, imagination is a faculty of the *mind*, the mind speaks for the soul, the soul is everywhere within us, *life* is everywhere within us, life ends in death, death makes us think of Heaven, Heaven is *above* the earth, the earth has several *oceans*, oceans are subject to storms, storms batter ships, ships need a good *captain*, a good captain has prudence, prudence is not found in young people, young people need to obey old people, old people like money, money makes people rich, rich people are not poor people, poor people know *necessity*, necessity makes people desperate, desperation knows no law, he who knows no law lives like a beast, *you* live like a beast, and this proves that you will be damned to Hell for all eternity!

DON JUAN
That was flawlessly reasoned.

SGANARELLE
If you don't give up your evil ways after *that*, then so much the worse for you.

(La Violette enters with Don Carlos.)

LA VIOLETTE
(To Don Juan) Monsieur...

SCENE 3

DON CARLOS
Don Juan, I have come to ask you what you have decided. You will remember that I took responsibility for resolving the matter which divides us, and that I am vitally concerned with the outcome. I must tell you, it is my fervent wish that we settle things peacefully, and there is nothing I wouldn't do to persuade you to take this course and publicly acknowledge my sister as your wife.

DON JUAN
Alas, I wish with all my heart I could give you the satisfaction you so understandably deserve, but Heaven expressly forbids that I do so. Through a long night and

day I have heard God's word and have been inspired
to change my life. I have no other thought now than to
cease and desist entirely from all worldly attachments,
to divest myself immediately of all forms of vanity, and
to emend, through the most sober and abstinent conduct,
all the criminal indulgences that tempted me in my blind,
wasted youth.

DON CARLOS

This change in you is not inconsistent with what I propose. The companionship of a lawful wife, especially
one so devout as my sister, can complement and help
sustain the praiseworthy intentions to which Heaven has
prompted you.

DON JUAN

And yet we *cannot* marry, for your sister has made the
same resolution as have I. She has chosen to retreat from
the world and return to the convent. We both have been
touched by God's grace, and at the same turn of events.

DON CARLOS

But alas her retreat cannot satisfy us, as it might be ascribed
to your humiliation of her and her family. Our honor dictates that she live with you by law and under God.

DON JUAN

I assure you though that this cannot be. I myself longed
for that happy union, but as I sought Heaven's consent
and blessing, a voice in my head cautioned me that I
mustn't dream any more of your sister, that for what I
had brought upon her I deserved not the reward of her
fellowship, but a much stricter expiation, and that I could
not be allowed to find salvation by her side.

DON CARLOS

Do you mean, Don Juan, to beguile us with beautiful
words?

DON JUAN

I am obeying the voice of God.

DON CARLOS

But can you expect me to leave here satisfied by such
words?

DON JUAN

It is not I but Heaven that expects it.

DON CARLOS

But you have forced my sister to betray her vows to that
same Heaven! How can you then abandon her?

DON JUAN

Heaven ordains our destinies.

DON CARLOS

And mine is to suffer this blot on our honor?

DON JUAN

Brother, you must look to God for an answer.

DON CARLOS

So it is all to be God's doing.

DON JUAN

That is the central tenet of Christian thought.

DON CARLOS

I understand you. I came in peace, and you do not wish
to respond in kind. I will meet you at dawn, you tell me
where.

DON JUAN

You must do what you must do. You know that I do not
lack courage, and that I know how to use my sword when
called upon. At first light I will take the little secluded street

behind the monastery on my way to matins, but I declare to you before God that I do not wish to fight you. If you attack me there, we shall see what God has planned for us.

DON CARLOS
Oh yes, we shall see. We shall see.

(Exit Don Carlos.)

SCENE 4

SGANARELLE
Oh worse than blasphemy! My God Monsieur, how can you be so…diabolical, your manner was so…unnerving! This new scam really *is* worse than all the others, I liked you much better the way you were before. I hoped and hoped that you'd be saved, but now I despair of it, in fact I think that God, who until now has indulged you—for He only knows what reason—will not be able to tolerate this latest atrocity!

DON JUAN
Come come, Heaven is not so vigilant or exacting as you like to believe. Think of all the heinous things that men have done in the name of Christ and that Heaven has overlooked!

(The specter of a woman appears to Don Juan and Sganarelle.)

SGANARELLE
Ah, Monsieur, Heaven is speaking to you. It is sending you a warning!

SPECTER
(Groaning) Ah…

DON JUAN

If Heaven wants to send me a warning, it will have to speak a little more clearly.

(Distant thunder sounds.)

SPECTER

Don Juan, you have but one fleeting moment to gain the forgiveness of God. If you do not repent here and now, you are finally and forever damned.

SGANARELLE

Do you hear, Monsieur?

DON JUAN

(To the specter) Who dares utter these words? I seem to recognize this voice…

SGANARELLE

It is a ghost, Monsieur, I can tell by the way it's walking.

DON JUAN

Ghost, phantom, devil—what is it *actually*? I want to know.

(He slashes at the specter with his sword. The specter vanishes, and a figure of Death appears in its place.)

SGANARELLE

Oh God! Look, Monsieur, it changed.

DON JUAN

(Interrupts) Nothing real can make me afraid. And what isn't real is imagined by man, and therefore ephemeral. Let's see if it has blood.

(He lunges at the figure with his sword. The figure disappears.)

SGANARELLE

(Clutching at Don Juan) Monsieur, you must give in to these signs!

DON JUAN

No—

SGANARELLE

(Interrupts) Throw yourself down and repent!

DON JUAN

No!

SGANARELLE

(Interrupts) It's your last chance!

DON JUAN

(Overlapping) No! Whatever happens, it will never be said of me that I apologized for my life.

(The Statue appears.)

SGANARELLE

Master, this is the end!

DON JUAN

(Overlapping) I shall never repent! Come, follow me—

STATUE

Stop Don Juan! Yesterday you gave me your word that you would dine with me.

DON JUAN

Lead the way!

STATUE

Give me your hand.

SGANARELLE

No!!

DON JUAN

(Seizing the Statue's hand) Ah!

(He cries out as the Statue grips his hand.)

STATUE

Don Juan! The anger of Heaven can no longer be contained. Sin without end, sin without remorse! Here is your agony, your death. Can you now deny the God who punishes you?

(The Statue releases Don Juan's hand. The earth opens into a fiery pit.)

DON JUAN

(Tearing at his shirt, overlapping the Statue) Oh Heaven, what is happening, I—What invisible fire consumes me? My flesh, I—*(Screaming)* Ah! I die! *(Screaming)* No—

(He is swallowed, screaming, into the fiery pit. Sganarelle throws himself down at the edge of the pit and cries out after Don Juan.)

SGANARELLE

Master! My wages! My wages! Master! Oh, everyone will be satisfied by your death—the Heaven you offended, the laws you violated, the creditors you dodged, the girls you deceived, the families you dishonored, the parents you demeaned, the women you ruined, the husbands you drove to the brink. Everyone's happy except me, with nothing in my pocket and nowhere to go! Oh Master! My wages, my wages! My wages.

(He breaks down. Lights fade to black.)
END OF PLAY

Restoring *Don Juan*

Stephen Wadsworth and Janice Paran

JANICE PARAN is a New Jersey-based writer and dramaturg. Formerly Director of Play Development at McCarter Theatre, she worked closely with Stephen Wadsworth as editor of his adaptation of *Don Juan* and as dramaturg for its first production at Seattle Repertory Theatre and the McCarter. She also worked in the same capacities on Wadsworth's series of plays by Pierre Carlet de Chamblain de Marivaux (1688-1763); on *Mirandolina*, his adaptation of Goldoni's *La Locandiera*; and on his adaptations of Beaumarchais' Figaro plays *Le Barbier de Séville* and *Le Mariage de Figaro*.

JP: Your translation and adaptation of *Don Juan* started out as a glint in the eye of the French scholar Joan DeJean, who had been a fan of your Marivaux adaptations and beseeched you to undertake a similar reclamation effort on behalf of Molière's famously problematic play. This was not, initially, an idea you warmed to. Why was that?

SW: I had read *Don Juan* only in translations, and the play had seemed dull to me, or at least it hadn't gripped or excited me. I'd found too little content in it, and practically none of the stylistic swagger and bubbling theatricality of Molière's verse plays or indeed of other 17th-century Parisian theater. I had a kind of theoretical interest in the play, and I had friends who were fond of it. We did two readings, at Seattle Repertory Theatre in 1999, of existing translations, and the actors were bored by the play and said so. Perhaps we should have exercised more imagination, but we weren't inspired. I went back to Joan with my tail between my legs and said, "Um, we did these readings, and I'm not getting it." And she said, "Well this is my whole point—the translations *are* boring, the received text is sometimes boring, but a lot of it wasn't written by Molière, and a lot of what he did write is gone, and what you have to do is re-imagine, re-*sense* the play through Molière's eyes—and I think if you used the Amsterdam text, you'd find clues. Now stop reading translations, and go look at the French."

JP: I want to ask you more about the Amsterdam text, but before we get to that: what finally turned you on to *Don Juan*—understanding what had been censored and why, or encountering Molière's own voice in the French language?

SW: Definitely the latter. I looked at page one of the French and was immediately captivated by Sganarelle and his language—and ashamed that for whatever reason I hadn't gone to the French months earlier. Of course, the dark tale of censorship had interested me, especially now that I had the sense from Joan that the received text was a feral cat that had been declawed, but I hadn't allowed myself to imagine just how severely censorship had hobbled the play.

Later, when I was working on it, I was most moved by the deeper implications of censorship, as Joan has defined them elsewhere in this volume. I was translating smack dab in the aftermath of 9/11 and the buildup to the wars in Afghanistan and Iraq, and I heard my own government rewriting history daily. Things that had been true yesterday were, officially, no longer true today; things that had meant one thing yesterday meant, officially, something else today. The government and the media, instead of reporting the news, were shaping and refashioning it. Which is precisely what Louis XIV's government had spent years doing to *Don Juan*. This baleful irony certainly inspired me to look harder for Molière's intention and to vindicate his political courage.

Another thing that turned me on about the project:

I'd had a strong sense of how the play might have looked and moved on the 17th-century stage, and this vision had been dancing in my head, very compellingly, ever since Joan first tried to tempt me. In fact, that strong sense (it felt like knowledge) of what the play's physicality must have been—of the extravagance and intensity of its style—made me want to look for the content that must originally have matched and filled that style.

JP: What was your immediate sense of Molière—Molière the writer as well as Molière the actor/practitioner—in reading the play in French for the first time?

SW: That first page of the play undoubtedly got to me not only because Sganarelle is such a delightful, dear, clever person, but also because Molière, in writing this role for himself to play, spoke directly through it. The person on that page is a servant being hounded to explain his master's immoral, cruel behavior; he takes refuge from his pursuer in a *lazzi*[8], a sort of stand-up riff, centering on snuff, a rich man's habit. But the snuff *lazzi* ends up getting him further into his central problem in the play—the inequities of society that separate him from his rich master—especially because the *lazzi* is fueled by his desperate need to be free of having to justify his master's base actions! Then in a further twist, he uses the snuff himself, and indeed speaks of passing it around to any and everyone, thereby appropriating the rich man's prerogative for persons of his own class. (In this adaptation he sums up with "Snuff is contagious, it brings all men together, which is probably why there are laws regulating its use.")

---

[8] Plural of *lazzo* (Italian), which may well be a transliteration of a dialect pronunciation of *laccio*, meaning a knot, or a bind; *lazzo* itself means a trick, a jest, a jibe, a drollery, and has now also come to mean a buffoonery of the kind practiced by *commedia dell'arte* players. The plural form is generally used as both singular and plural in English. A *lazzi* is a short vaudeville routine developed around a dilemma in the play, often in which the characters involved get stuck in the dilemma, or in an attempt to solve it.

Sganarelle cannot escape his troubles, though in making immediate contact with the audience he quickly hooks them, with that protean, can-do charm from his Italian *commedia dell'arte* ancestors. And he carries this forward with him into the free-thinking fray of Don Juan's actions and motives: Molière positions himself, the character he played, and his audience at a critical remove from the anti-hero *Don Juan,* but it is clear in everything he says that Sganarelle admires, perhaps even loves his master, and that he is grateful for the amazing opportunity he has been given by his master to debate freely, to use his reason, to question anything—even things off-limits to a person of his master's station, to say nothing of his own.

And last, a short way into that first scene, I was startled to read, in Sganarelle's description of his master, almost the same words I had just read in a document written not six months earlier than the play—only this time they were written about Molière himself. In August of 1664 Pierre Roullé, a prominent cleric, published an homage to Louis XIV, praising him for prohibiting performances of *Tartuffe*. Look at the two descriptions:

> Roullé on Molière, August 1664: "…a man, or rather a demon in the flesh and resembling a man, the most notably impious creature and libertine who ever lived."

> Molière/Sganarelle on Don Juan, February 1665: "…the single most vile miscreant that the world has ever produced: a dangerous man, a dog, a demon…"

My hair stood on end. Molière had seen Roullé's tribute (in which Roullé had also recommended that Moliére be burned at the stake) and dared to spit it directly back at him, in a form no less public than Roullé's, in fact probably much more so. Molière's intentions in *Don Juan* could no longer be doubted.

But then I also had a vivid impression of the language,

too: direct, unfussy, juicy, very much not *poised*—in the sense that even the servants in the verse plays are poised on the prosody and crisp on the rhymes. Well. That was my immediate sense of Molière as writer and as actor/practitioner. Painful ironies, indefatigable hope, the necessary sharpening of wits. It's the Enlightenment in formation.

JP: What were Molière's intentions in *Don Juan*? What have we been missing?

SW: It has become clear to me that the original *Don Juan* was one of the most trenchant, well-aimed works of political theater in Western European history. It was also a ripping entertainment, one of Molière's greatest popular successes, but only when its political content is brought back to the fore can we really see the whole picture. There are many deceptively naïve gestures in the play (they had deceived me)—the peasant and pastoral elements, the delight in the supernatural, the plain-spoken prose text (*Don Juan* alone of Molière's great plays is not in verse), the parodies of Corneille's "high-brow" characters—but when they set the stage for Molière's slashing aperçus and become the medium for Don Juan's remorseless world-view, they take on new life.

What have we been missing? Not only the actual text, but all those years of engaging with it are lost. Louis' censors succeeded in killing Molière's text forever. One of the most insidious forms of censorship was probably actual rewriting. Imagine: the typesetter takes his trays of set type to the censor. The censor then removes lines and paragraphs here and there but doesn't like to inconvenience the poor typesetter and so invents new text, more in line with his own views of what the characters should say. And the typesetter then fills the empty spaces in his tray with the censor's deathless prose. And I do mean deathless, because that's part of what we've been calling *Don Juan* ever since. So it's not just what we've been missing that we have to question, it's what we've been hearing.

JP: All of which relates to the political content you've mentioned. Who exactly was Molière's *Don Juan* in relation to Louis XIV's France?

SW: He was a free-thinking outsider criticizing the way society worked. Throughout the 17th century, France, the most populous and educated of the Western European states, was becoming increasingly aware of rationalism—the philosophy that reason, *intellect*, was the key to knowledge, rather than the senses or passions or religious dogma. Rational thinking was very exciting in theory. But the minute you prove that one organism is essentially like another, that organisms within a species are essentially equal in some sense, you might realize that human beings, say, are all essentially equal as well. Take that thought one step further, and you start questioning everything about a society that doesn't treat all human beings equally. Suddenly rational thinking is scary and threatening. And if you're running a religion used to determining how men should imagine their world, a religion that has cozied up to a classist, racist government of the privileged few, why then you have a serious dilemma facing you. We know reason finally got the better of ancien-régime France in the bloody end of the 18th century, but here's Don Juan in 1665, unnerving censors and audiences with his rational, logical, unapologetic world-view. The biggest surprise to me in working on this play was watching Don Juan's skeptical, prove-it-to-me mind crash through the wall of the 17th century and march into the Age of Enlightenment, full of prescience and anger and awe-inspiring intellectual confidence.

JP: But wasn't the play considered risqué in its time primarily because of Don Juan's sexual adventuring? Can Don Juan be a *provocateur* for us in the same way he was for 17th-century French audiences?

SW: I don't think sex had anything to do with the play's censorship. I can't imagine that anyone in the first audience found it shocking that an aristocrat would seduce a peasant girl. There may have been a few evolved minds, or upwardly mobile middle-class folk, who saw it as censure of the heedless aristocracy, but such seduction scenes were stock scenes in life and on the stage. The fact that Don Juan had stolen into a convent and seduced and abandoned a *nun* may have raised a few eyebrows: it's the first hint of what he's after in the play, but the censors didn't pick up on it. What he's after was the problem for them—the separation of church and state, hypocrisy in church and state, rational thinking versus religious doctrine. Now, if you said some of the things Don Juan says at a town barbecue in early 21st-century America, you would be considered at *least* a *provocateur*, probably worse. At the moment we live in a country that in some areas bans books, outlaws the teaching of science, denies climate change, and pushes to entrench religious doctrine in legislation. And when I was working on the play our then president (George W. Bush) was a man who, like Louis XIV, was strongly influenced by the religious right, and was said to believe his decisions were divine in origin. Don Juan can be a *provocateur* for us in very much the same way he was for his original audience, yes. And you don't have to be a liberal Democrat to agree with him, either: his great hypocrisy speech rings loud and clear to anyone who's leery of the way politics are conducted in our nation's capital. The play would probably thrill a Donald Trump rally. When we played it in Washington, D.C., we had politicians from both sides of the aisle present and laughing.

JP: Talk about the end of the play. Is Don Juan's demise the only possible 17th-century outcome? What do we do with that ending today, if we're more inclined to view Don Juan as a rebel hero? Or is that a big mistake?

SW: Well, Molière's Don Juan was too probing for Louis XIV's France, wasn't he. I think if Molière hadn't killed

Don Juan for his sins, the play wouldn't have gotten onstage at all. By killing him, and making the play seem like a cautionary tale (free thinkers meet a terrible fate), he bought himself a forum in which to speak the ideas of the play—and ideas, once spoken publicly, are forever alive, unkillable. Molière was undoubtedly trying to buy himself a forum in which to *continue* to speak, too, by dealing his anti-hero this particular death—a *Heaven-ordained* hand dragging the Don away to a merciless death with no hope of salvation.

I don't think it's wrong to think of Don Juan as a rebel hero, but even if we do, we don't necessarily think that he's going to get off scot-free, do we? I'm sure there are plenty of people in our audiences[9] who see Don Juan as a hero, and who are dismissive of his *deus ex machina* demise. Well, there are various ways the statue's appearance might be played if an interpreter felt it necessary to move away from the idea of *divine* retribution, but there's no getting around the fact that Molière's statue comes and takes Don Juan to his death. There's no way Molière could have let Don Juan live.

JP: How do our received notions about Don Juan (the legend, not the Molière play), whatever their source, predispose us to hear the play?

SW: The words Don Juan are a catch phrase for notions of sexual prowess, lady killing and bad morals. The 2000 American Heritage Dictionary's first definition of a Don Juan, for example, was "A libertine, a profligate." Their 2014 edition says, "A man who seduces or attempts to seduce women as a matter of habit." So some audience members assume that Don Juan should be obviously attractive physically and/or morally corrupt. And most audience members don't make much of a differentiation among the various Don Juans they may have heard about or know—

---

[9] The first production of this adaptation played in Seattle, San Diego, Washington, D.C., and Princeton, New Jersey.

Tirso de Molina's, Molière's, Mozart and Da Ponte's, Byron's, Shaw's (although some make the mistake of expecting Molière's to be just like their idea of Mozart's, or Mozart's just like Byron's). But in fact these artists each used the Don Juan archetype to different ends and at different moments in cultural and social history. Molière's Don Juan is dangerous and sexy first and foremost because of his *mind*, and our audiences have been surprised to meet a character significantly more brainy and substantive than they expected, surprised to be preoccupied and entertained principally by his *arguments*, and to a lesser extent by his exploits with women. He's an archetype of social anarchy, just as much as of sexual glamour, and that's why all these artists gravitate toward him: he's a reliable mouthpiece for people who need to rail against a norm, explode a fallacy, or float an iffy new idea.

"Libertine," like "liberal," derives from "liber," the Latin word for freedom—and also, delightfully, for *book* (or as my first Latin dictionary put it so poetically, "any writing consisting of several leaves"). "Libertine" and "liberal" have noble roots, but like many words describing people who question the status quo, they have been relegated to the land of invective.[10]

JP: Doesn't the notion of a freethinker seem rather quaint today, given the permissiveness of our culture? Yet you've resisted updating, transplanting Don Juan.

SW: America at large, at the beginning of the 21st century, couldn't easily be called permissive, do you think? We're

---

[10] In 17th-century France the word "libertin" (libertine) described someone who thought freely or independently, particularly about religion. It later came to describe someone unusually free of convention or standard patterns of behavior—the sexual connotation evolved in the 18th century. Sganarelle, our man on the street, defines libertines in this adaptation of the play as "men who think they're above the law, who lack sufficient respect for these sacred things or who disobey the Commandments." But Don Juan doesn't hold sacred what the church has decided he should, and therefore doesn't actually respect the Commandments, or laws that are in bed with the dictates of the church. One of the points he makes is that we ought not to let our minds be made up for us by any kind of predisposition.

in a quite intolerant phase now, with about half the nation embracing a narrow world-view, high on personal gain, lower on core freedoms. I think the idea of a freethinker who flouts convention, honor and law is bound to be fresh in pretty much any era, and he ought to be quite arresting in 2015, 2035 or 2085. If we are a permissive culture it's because we are a complacent culture—we *permit* events to occur without exercising our right to *determine* them. It is into this complacency that extremists have always stepped. Molière took stock of this very trend for us back there in the summer and fall of 1665. We presented the play first in 2002, two years into an evolving Bush *fils* presidency and shortly after 9/11, then again in 2004, when, emboldened by the opportunities of 9/11, the Bush regime had made its intentions clear and was facing re-election. We noticed a huge difference in audience response to the politics of the play. There were frequent gasps, snorts, sighs and other noises of recognition. These were the days of the first Abu Ghraib prison scandal of the Iraq War, and Defense Secretary Donald Rumsfeld was briefly under attack from all sides. A *New York Times* headline photo showed Rumsfeld surrounded by Bush, Cheney and Co. They all faced in one direction while Rumsfeld looked at the camera from the center of this tight, protective group that was rallying to his defense. Listening to Don Juan's hypocrisy speech that night was a pretty rich experience, and there was nothing quaint about it, to use your word:

> "This is exactly how I shall now protect my interests, exempting myself from any further censure and actually enhancing my reputation. Everyone will be happy. I won't give up a single one of my cherished pursuits, but I'll take care to indulge myself covertly and with a minimum of noise, and if anyone finds me out I'll call on my cabal, unworried and unhurried, and those terribly pious friends will immediately close ranks and vindicate my name."

JP: It's easy to see why Shaw was attracted to Don Juan; he is a freethinker after Shaw's own heart.

SW: Shaw and Don Juan were both freethinkers, that's true, but their like-mindedness goes deeper—they both train their beady, agnostic eyes on a specific moment in time and analyze the cross section of society that lives there. Shaw lays bare, or at least notices, every fallibility of the social contract with unquenchable curiosity and enthusiasm. He and Don Juan see and think clearly, so they tell us the whole story about those moments—we get from both of them finely calibrated readings on politics, religion, class and sex. Shaw's biographer Michael Holroyd wrote about Shaw in words that perfectly describe Molière in *Don Juan*: "Shaw will not allow complacency; he hates second-hand opinions; he attacks fashion; he continually challenges and unsettles, questioning and provoking us even when he is making us laugh." Shaw himself wrote, in the epistolary preface to *Man and Superman* (his Don Juan play), "But my conscience is the genuine pulpit article: it annoys me to see people comfortable when they ought to be uncomfortable; and I insist on making them think in order to bring them to conviction of sin. If you don't like my preaching you must lump it. I really cannot help it." Which could have come out of the mouth of Molière's Don Juan.

JP: Let's talk specifically about the 1683 Amsterdam text and why Joan DeJean's edition of it matters.

SW: The Amsterdam text is a French-language edition published in Holland in 1683, outside the purview of the French censors. It matters because there was an edition published in France (obviously *within* the purview of the French censors) only a year earlier, and a comparison of the two editions is revealing.

JP: *Don Juan*—as originally written—had exactly one performance in 1665 before the censors got to it, and only lasted a few more before it was pulled from the repertoire, never to be produced again in Molière's lifetime. So subsequent French productions—even at the "official" national theater, the Comédie Française—were based on bowdlerized versions of the play.

SW: Exactly. No original Molière manuscript exists, we assume that improvisation in performance somewhat altered the original written text, we know that memorial reconstruction played a role in the making of editions (actors, auditors and critics scribbling what they heard during performances), and censors repeatedly altered the text. So we can't be sure of the provenance of *any* edition of this play. The challenge is therefore to determine which of the sources is the most authentic. The argument for the Amsterdam text is strong. Henri Wetstein, the Dutchman who originally published it, was probably given a manuscript by someone who had first-hand knowledge of the original, who disapproved of the French edition of 1682 and wanted a more accurate text in print. That person might have been an actor, or someone connected to Molière's family, but sometimes I wonder if it mightn't even have been a French government official—someone like Nicolas de La Reynie, the head of the Parisian police, who we believe owned one of the less censored copies. In any case, the possibility that the person in charge of book censorship might have been responsible for saving a controversial text is an irony too delicious not to ponder. It's certainly an irony that puts its finger on certain contradictions of Louis' France.

JP: Is it really so surprising that the play was bowdlerized—considering, for instance, that numerous "improved" versions of Shakespeare's plays held the English stage for centuries?

SW: I guess it's not surprising, no, but the English have made it their business to make up for lost time with exhaustive scholarship about Shakespeare and virtually every aspect of his work as writer, producer and actor. The French are behind in the cross-examination of sources. When I spoke about Marivaux on a mostly French panel in New York some years ago, I chose to address his collaborative relationship with the Italian troupe for whom he wrote his plays. The picture I painted of how that worked, all of it based on research readily available in France, shocked several members of the panel, notably including the artistic director of the Comédie Française at the time, who rebutted strenuously that what I'd said was "discutable," debatable, and that it was "inappropriate" to suggest that Marivaux wasn't first and only a French artist in the great French tradition.

JP: But contemporary editors of Molière's plays in France and elsewhere have surely used the Amsterdam text as a resource before now.

SW: Yes, but only by integrating bits of it into the 1682 French text. What happened to the *original* text, or more accurately what that text may have been, is one of the great literary mysteries of European letters. Joan wanted to find out more, and in her quest got the Amsterdam edition published in French for the first time since 1683, though not, it is interesting to note, by a French publisher. One French publisher called it an "edition gauchiste" (leftist!), the idea being that it was unthinkable to challenge the accepted text, or to publish an edition claiming that the French continued to be complicit in the censorship of a masterpiece. She eventually found a publisher outside the country (Droz, in Switzerland) who didn't hesitate—a scenario vividly recalling the 1683 Amsterdam publication itself.

JP: Is it really radically different from other editions of *Don Juan* that have incorporated some of its material?

SW: No, at least not to look at it. It's perhaps 88% the same as the 1682 edition, but the differences are substantive and suggestive. The Pauper scene (Act III, Scene 2), in which Don Juan tempts a pious hermit with a valuable gold coin (the louis d'or, named for Louis' own father, the previous king), had been cut after the first performance in 1665, and it was again quashed in 1682, and this, it can easily be argued, is the central scene in the play, lying as it does exactly half-way through the text and providing the turning point for both action and tone. It's there in the Amsterdam edition. This is the biggest chunk of restored text.

There are many places where there are differences of a word or a phrase, and often these immediately precede or follow a passage that felt to me, as I worked along through the logic of action and character, somehow jarring, different in tone, diction or flow (if you will) from what followed or came before. I began to feel that in some of these cases the small differences in the Amsterdam were, in effect, knife marks—that these were places where censors, over the years, may have cut into the play. So in fact the 1683 Amsterdam text, in these instances, may not have been offering up answers or lines any truer than the 1682 French text, but the differences between the two often show, I feel, where controversial material originally lay. They're clues. Joan's point was: it's time for us to make something of these clues, and more than sheer (or mere!) scholarship is required to help us imagine what was heard in that 1665 premiere.

JP: In crafting your adaptation, how did you balance a desire for authenticity—particularly given the play's slippery provenance—with your impulses to revise or invent material? And in what ways, specifically, did you underline or enhance ideas that might have been implicitly understood in 1665 but which might need heightening for contemporary audiences?

SW: Again, we know that what we have isn't the original text, so authenticity as far as textual integrity is moot.

But the Amsterdam text seemed like the most useful tool with which to explore the play. Ultimately, I made a sort of reconstruction of the original performance, and understanding something of the styles of utterance, gesture and presentation in Molière's theater helped me in imagining how the text might have moved.

The theatrical conventions, the style of playing, the world of design, the intellectual and political climate at court, the evolving emergence of a middle class, the memoirs and sketches of theatrical and social life, the music and its encyclopedia of manners and emotion—these are all things about which much is known and thought. When I felt they were alive and current in me, I took on this project, and then I did my level best to be a sensitive vessel.

I allowed myself to write into those cracks left, as I suspected, by the knife, to explore where Molière might have been headed. Sometimes this didn't seem right, sometimes it did. I frequently allowed Don Juan to go on talking about what we know were the contentious issues. Sometimes he had just a little more to say. There's almost nothing changed in his Act I, Scene 2 speech to Sganarelle about his compulsions to seduce women, but after the play turns, in the Pauper scene, I let him push through occasionally to an edgier place. In Act III, Scene 5, he says of the Viceroy's statue:

My my, isn't he handsome all dressed up as a sort of emperor *crusading for the cross. You know, it's curious how human beings want to be remembered as kings. I wonder if kings want to be remembered as human beings.*

The text in italics is new.

I want contemporary audiences to understand how high the stakes were in that theater at the 1665 premiere, with Molière reeling from the scandal of *Tartuffe* (engineered by a right-wing religious group, the Compagnie du Saint-Sacrement) and clearly determined to continue speaking out. I've added a number of gestures to explicate this essential aspect of the text—for one example, a verse prologue addressing the circumstances of the first performance, and for another, the repetition throughout the play of the prologue's salvo, "Long live the king," which is offered by various characters, on the spur of the moment, when the text gets dangerous, mentioning the king in a dubious context, or directly challenging the people who would have been in that first audience (members of Saint-Sacrement, censors, representatives and courtiers of Louis XIV if indeed not the King himself).

And yes, I did some contextualizing so that audiences today will understand clearly ideas that would have been implicitly understood by audiences then—medical issues, blasphemy, class differences in a number of spots through the play, and dueling and the dictates of honor. For example, in Act III, Scene 3, Don Carlos now says:

> My brother and I, compelled by one of those vexatious and sensitive matters of honor, must stay on the outskirts and wait for our prey. It is distressing that such matters oblige one to sacrifice one's family name, perhaps even one's own life, but honor is a rigorous taskmaster. *What irony, that honor often compels us to fight our adversaries to the death, but that dueling is now forbidden.*

Again, the text in italics is new.

JP: In your versions of the Marivaux plays you added some material for the "Italian" comics, Harlequin and Trivelin. Have you done that in *Don Juan*?

SW: I have done some of that, yes. Molière, clearly an awesome onstage farceur himself, shared two Parisian theaters several years earlier with Tiberio Fiorelli's *commedia* troupe and is reported to have studied with Fiorelli (known as Scaramouche). They played alternate nights on the same boards, watched each other from the wings, and poached liberally on each other's terrain for material, bits and style—this Italian-French connection was a stylistic intermarriage that elated Parisian audiences for at least a century. Under Molière's rigorous tutelage the French actors absorbed the improvisational freedom of the Italians. I recognized their inclination to improvise, especially Molière/Sganarelle's, and allowed them to riff now and then, and not always innocently. The Italians' improvisational freedom led them regularly into politically subversive waters. In 1697 Louis banished them for making fun of Madame de Maintenon (his second wife, and a quite pious lady). It's important to remember here that Sganarelle's text in this play was often as shocking to the original audience as Don Juan's, though not for all the same reasons.[11]

For example, I added an elaborate food lazzi in Act IV just before the Statue first arrives, and the ongoing coin-purse vaudeville during the Don Juan-Carlos scene in Act 3. The received text has the magnificent lazzi in which Don Juan sweet-talks two women at once (II, 4); I've often wondered if that was part of what Molière originally wrote down. When the original celluloid is found of the live telecast from 1665, with Molière's original text, I will eat an actual hat if we find that Sganarelle's text was spoken as it was first written.

JP: You've also retained some of the *Don Juan* material that has come down to us from other versions of the text.

SW: I call the play *Don Juan*, not *The Stone Feast* or any other translation of Molière's alternate title. I retain the longer version of the Carlos-Alonso scene, including the informative satirical, discourse about honor which the Amsterdam text abjures. And I do send Don Juan to hell through a flame-spitting trap door (that stage direction, added by scandal-wary editors, is not in the Amsterdam edition). The theatricality of the gesture appeals to me, and I think it clarifies the absoluteness of his fate without

---

[11] See Appendix 2

167

necessarily altering the point of view of play or production. In any case, Molière kills Don Juan, just not with trap door and flames.

This version of *Don Juan* isn't the Amsterdam text translated, it is a version of the play based on a comparison of Amsterdam 1683 and Paris 1682, a version that aims to imagine the original text and the high-risk circumstances of its first, doomed performance.

JP: What happened, exactly, to Molière's original text of the play may be one of the theater's enduring mysteries, but an even greater one to me is how Molière managed to be both robustly critical of French society under Louis XIV and a great favorite of the king's.

SW: Louis loved beautiful things and seems to have respected the people who made them—the fabric on his chair, the person who wove it, and the Lyon silk trade that produced it. He wanted the best craftsmen to fashion and amplify his world, he loved the theater, and Molière had been delighting him for some time. I think he really liked Molière, as a person as well as a man of the theater. The excerpts of *Tartuffe* that played Versailles in 1664 probably embarrassed rather than shocked the Saint-Sacrement cabal, and they sprang into action. They were a powerful lobby at court, Molière was an occasional visitor. They couldn't prevail in blocking the Versailles *Tartuffe*, but they did in leveraging Louis to suppress it thereafter. Yet the king then allowed Molière to produce *Don Juan* in Paris, and to continue presenting it, albeit in a revised version, after the censors pounced on the premiere. Five weeks of that, and the play was gone: apparently Louis had been, eventually, persuaded by the lobbyists to remove it from circulation. I don't have much sense of Louis being a moral force at this phase of his life; somewhat later the influence of his more sober helpmeet, Madame de Maintenon, seems to have curbed his appetite for worldly pleasures. I think the suppression of *Don Juan*, and of Molière, was purely political. Perhaps it pained Louis, we don't know. I can't imagine he thought about it for long. It certainly pained Molière. I shouldn't wonder if he never recovered from it.

Also, we have to remember that Molière *gradually* grew critical of the social contract, his earlier plays were not characterized by the blend of tart, acerbic wit and extremely edgy content that characterizes the three great plays of this period—*Tartuffe, Don Juan, The Misanthrope*.

JP: Has *Don Juan* influenced your assessment of Molière— does it shed light on other of his plays?

SW: I can't look at *Tartuffe* or *The Misanthrope* now except through *Don Juan*'s eyes. I feel that each successive play is built not only on the perceptions and convictions of its predecessor, but also on Molière's experience of writing its predecessor and watching it explode on contact with society. I think *Don Juan* is a cry from a deep place in Molière the citizen and man, and perhaps *The Misanthrope* comes from an even deeper place: Alceste turns away from society and stews in an existential grief, highly critical but now impotent in a way that the opportunist Tartuffe and the outlaw Don Juan were not. It's a kind of trilogy, a gradual turning away and inside, an angry descent of the spirit, and there's a terrible sadness at the end. Perhaps it's the story of Molière's final disillusionment, it can't be far off. Seen this way, these plays are ripe for re-examination. They aren't just clever, they aren't just cutting, they aren't just edgy, they are full of heartbreak. But Americans are easily fooled by rhyme and shows of merriness. I think Richard Wilbur's translations of the verse plays are absolutely spectacular, but our performance tradition for them tends to be either unremittingly jolly in an insistently shallow way or unremittingly grim in a determinedly post-modern way.

JP: As was the case with your Marivaux adaptations, it's a little difficult to separate your work as writer from your directorial vision. A Stephen Wadsworth production carries with it a particular audio-visual universe that is steeped in, dependant upon, sustained by the staging conventions and cultural references of the play's own period. Talk about some of those conventions and why you made use of them in your production.

SW: The first thing I knew when I started to engage with this play was how it would look if I directed it. After Seattle Rep asked me to make this version, and even before I knew that I could, I spoke to the Rep staff about what I saw: dark, deep wooden proscenium; beautifully painted flats that flew; heavy use of footlights; lavish and detailed period clothing; a lot of direct address to the audience; highly theatrical use of voice and gesture; music by Molière's contemporaries, probably Lully and Marais. I knew that these things—each of them a convention of Molière's theater—would guide me towards the heart of the play. I believe that style encodes content, I mentioned it earlier here, and you and I have discussed this at length elsewhere [see *Marivaux: Three Plays*, Smith and Kraus, 1999]. I also envisioned the company on the stage at the beginning, with the senior actor addressing the audience in a verse prologue. That was about finding a 17th-century gesture for some deft contextualizing, but also about setting up for the audience the world of Molière's actors, the stakes for them at the first performance, and the very audience-conscious style in which they played.

Direct address is particularly important, and revealing. Before the intimacy of film encouraged actors to play scenes directly to one another, most actors, everywhere, felt their responsibility was to communicate to the *audience* how they felt about their scene partner. Things were played *out*, so the audience could see the faces, which of course implied contact with the audience. That was the way actors made their thoughts and feelings available to the audience, but given that, it became a vessel for communicating other essences of the play, indeed an invitation to engage with the audience *about* the play. Through this engagement with the crowd a character might enlist the audience's sympathy for his or her point of view and strengthen his status in the scene at hand. Here is a world of theatrical possibility utterly lost to actors who play, say, the Pauper scene, directly to one another. Don Juan and Sganarelle, whose ongoing dialogue about big issues is the spine of *Don Juan*, originally spoke much more to their audience than to each other, I am convinced. They vied for the intellectual, emotional and theatrical sympathies of their audience with oratorical skills, with seductive physical ingenuity, and with *charm*—these were attributes of the actor rather than of the character, and were used to hook an audience on their characters' arguments rather than to build a character who was content to remain behind the fourth wall in a self-contained reality.

The actors in our production had to learn how to think as the *actors* they were representing, as well as the characters they played for Molière. And direct address and the "improvised" moments in this text often signal moments when they are *actors* responding to the intensity or danger of a scene, as it happens (such as when they say "Long live the King"). This was a thrilling tool to use in reconstructing, if you will, this text. And it makes for some risky, wild moments in the theater which could not be further removed from the television realism of many contemporary American plays.

JP: Do you have a mandate for other directors interested in doing this *Don Juan*?

SW: No, I welcome directorial approaches different from my own, for one thing because I, as writer, then have opportunities to gauge the strength of the script itself. Plus different directorial approaches are part of a healthy theater diet. We were speaking of Shaw earlier—did you ever see that great sentence he wrote in a preface to—

171

oh irony!— *The Philanderer*? "All the attempts within my experience to modernize ancient plays have only produced worse anachronisms than those they aimed at remedying." Perfectly said, *that's* the issue. I do enjoy a smart updating, but I wish modern theatrical freethinkers all had Shaw's integrity and rigor.

Also, by thinking in a pre-modern rather than post-modern way about pre-modern plays, we can rediscover how out-and-out gobsmackingly thrilling modernity itself was when it crested the hill. Post-modernism is a dodgy platform for a curator of pre-modern art, but interpreters should look through whatever lens they feel they must. It's just that the theater of the baroque is A) a rich and beautiful landscape as it is, B) already so complex and encoded that another lens can confuse our sense of the original intent, and C) too rarely glimpsed in its own guise not to be done, occasionally, on its own aesthetic terms.

All directors should, at some point in their careers, make it their honor-bound and pleasure-bound business to learn the history of the play at hand and its author, and to steep themselves in the aesthetic world of its time. "Ça vaut le voyage," as the French guidebook used to say—it's worth the visit.

On December 16, 1664, Molière's troupe, who had commissioned settings for Don Juan from the painters Jean Simon and Pierre Prat, approved and accepted them. The contract, from December 3, sets forth the painting order and the terms.

> *Contract for painting work for the honorable actors of His Lordship the Duke of Orléans, the only brother of the King.*
>
> *First a palace, consisting of five flats on each side, through which one will see two flats of the sea and a façade all the way upstage. The first of these frames shall reach a height of 18 feet, with all the others growing smaller in perspective. Then a hamlet in a leafy setting, consisting of five flats on each side, the first 18 feet high, with all the others growing smaller, in perspective, and a grotto covering the back wall, through which one will see two flats and an upstage vista, both of the ocean.*
>
> *Then a forest, consisting of three flats on each side, of which the first will be 18 feet high and the others growing smaller, and an upstage frame that opens on which will be painted a sort of temple surrounded by greenery.*
>
> *Then the interior of the temple, consisting of five flats on each side, of which the first set shall be 18 feet high, and the others growing smaller, and a frame that opens, against the upstage wall, depicting the far end of the temple.*
>
> *Then a room, consisting of three flats on each side, of*

which the first will be 18 feet high, with the others growing smaller, and a final frame depicting the upstage wall of the room.

Then a town, consisting of five flats on either side, of which the first will be 18 feet high, with the others growing smaller. The third of the five will depict the town gate; and the two smallest sets of flats as well as the background tableau depicting the town.

Further, four cloth border strips depicting sky, spanning the width of the stage.

Further, four cloth border strips depicting a frieze of arches spanning the width of the stage.[12]

Further, a hung piece depicting two columns downstage, with a cloth border strip above depicting a frieze, to form a proscenium.

Further, two small balconies at the sides downstage, which belong to the acting company and need to be repainted.

Further, the existing hung ceiling must be repainted.

The actors shall provide the workers with built flats covered with canvas, as well as platforms, all ready to be painted.

The document ends as follows:

The painters shall work without interruption in order to finish everything perfectly within six weeks, starting on the day on which said flats, canvases and platforms shall be provided, for a fee of three hundred livres deposit, which the commissioners promise to pay should they not provide the abovementioned materials. The acting company shall provide the painters with a working space as appropriate. The total fee shall come to approximately nine hundred livres, which sum the acting company solemnly promises to pay the painters as follows: three hundred livres at the beginning of the work, three hundred livres in the middle of the work, and the remaining three hundred livres to be paid when the work shall be accomplished

---

[12] Of these sets of borders above the stage, the first was surely the largest in scale, and the others growing less and less wide, in diminishing perspective, like the flats they joined.

to the perfect satisfaction of the commissioners,
and to the approval of experts and connoisseurs.

The original document has several changes marked in ink
and initialed by Molière "J.B.P.M"—Jean Baptiste Poquelin
Molière. His name appears at the top of the list of signatories,
which also includes those of the painters Simon and Prat and
of four other members of the troupe, including Charles Varlet
La Grange, who created the role of Don Juan. There are so
many spelling errors and inconsistencies and mistakes[13] in
the original of this handwritten document that it is easy to
see how the text of *Don Juan*, transcribed at speed during
performances by people of varying degrees of literacy, could
quickly lose its integrity.

Exactly six months later, after the signing of this document, Molière's daughter by Arminde, Esprit-Madeleine,
was baptized. The only of his children who survived him,
she died in 1723.

---

[13] In one iteration of the repeated phrase "of which the first will be 18 feet
high," for example the document says "18 inches."

On December 13, 1678, after a series of performances of *Don Juan* by a provincial troupe, a case against the play and its players was argued and judged by the Faculty of Theology at the Sorbonne. Argument and judgment were published in Paris in 1733, as part of the entry on theater, in the lightly titled *The Dictionary of Cases of Conscience Decided According to Moral Principles, the Customs of the Church, the Authority of Prelates and Doctors, and the Jurisprudence of the Realm.*

The following are brief selections, first from the Argument, then from the Judgment.

From the Argument

> *This play is pernicious and full of impiety; not only does it enact the most horrible vices, it also teaches how to commit them.*
>
> *The actor who plays the atheist character openly mocks God, and his scoundrel valet, who seems to take the part of religion and to defend virtue, comports himself in a manner so impertinent and jesting that all his speeches amount to further mockery.*
>
> *The topic of this play and the manner in which it is treated are loathsome.*
>
> *It is true that the atheist is punished in the end, but the author's goal is to entertain and amuse the spectators, as he states in his preface, and*

not to inspire in them a proper horror of ungodliness and crime.

After having been warned by the Church that they shouldn't present this play, and after absolution was refused to a woman who had appeared onstage with them, the actors complained to their patrons about the warning, and furthermore made public jest of it—some seeking to excuse themselves by passing responsibility to the patrons who had paid them to perform. The question is thus whether absolution should be refused to all of them until they promise to mend their ways, and promise not to perform the play any more and to exact the same promise from their patrons. For if they only discuss it with the patrons and pass along the decision to them, can they really be granted absolution?

From the Judgment

The Doctors of Theology in Paris, who have considered the case laid out here, are of the opinion that the sacraments cannot be administered to those who perform, or allow to be performed, the play entitled The Stone Guest; they believe them to be unworthy, as they would accomplices to a crime. It is indeed the constant doctrine of the Church that no Christian is allowed to present or encourage, even as a spectator at a performance, theatrical works full of amorous intrigues and impiety.

Saint Cyprien[14], in his De Spectaculis [On Public Presentations], wrote: "In the theater one learns about adultery by seeing it; and a woman who was chaste when walking into the performance, through the contagion of publicly

---

[14] A wealthy pagan Carthaginian in the third century B.C.E. who converted to Christianity, became a bishop, and wrote frequently and with eloquence, in Latin, on a number of moral and religious issues.

authorized evil, walks out of it corrupted and vulnerable to promiscuity. To what degree are the gestures and actions of the players capable of defiling the heart, inspiring debauchery, feeding vice and licentiousness? Is there a single person who would not be shaken by such a dangerous sight? The sensibility, convictions and virtue, even of the most devout, are often weakened and reversed in the theater.

Generally, French names are accented on the final syllable.

DON JUAN is probably best pronounced fairly simply—DAWN *WAHN*—and not with a Spanish accent or in the English fashion (*DAWN JEW-EN*), at least in North America.

The other characters are:

GUSMAN	GOOZ-*MAHN*
SGANARELLE	ZGAHN-UH-*RELL*
DONNA ELVIRA	*DAWN*-UH EL-*VEE*-RUH
PIERROT	PEE-AIR-*OH*
CHARLOTTE	SHAR-*LAWT*
MATHURINE	MAT-EUR-*EEN*
LA RAMÉE	LAH RAH-*MAY*
DON CARLOS	DAWN *CAR*-LOHSS
DON ALONSO	DAWN AH-*LAWN*-SOH
RAGOTIN	RAH-GOH-*TA(N)*
LA VIOLETTE	LAH VYOH-*LET*
MONSIEUR DIMANCHE	M'SYER DEE-*MAW(N)SH*
DON LUIS	DAWN LOO-*EESS*

Constantly appearing are:

Madame	MAH-*DAHM*
Monsieur	M'*SYE(R)*

"**Madame**" should be pronounced *à la française*, with the stress on the second syllable.

In the Prologue, the Speaker addresses:

Mesdames	MAY-_DAHM_
Messieurs	MESS-_SYE(R)_

And he also mentions:

LeVau	L'_VOH_
LeBrun	L'_BRUH(N)_
Le Nôtre	L'_NOH_-TR(UH)
Versailles	VAIR-_SIGH_

In I,1 SGANARELLE refers to:

Sardanapalus	SAR-DAH-_NAH_-PUH-LUSS
Epicurus	EP-IH-_CURE_-US

In I,2 DON JUAN says:

bien touché	BYA(N) TOO-_SHAY_

And also:

sur mer	SEER _MAIR_

In II,1 Pierrot mentions:

Tomasina	TOH-MAH-_SEE_-NAH

In II,2 CHARLOTTE mentions her aunt:

Simonetta	SEE-MOH-_NET_-UH

In III,3 DON CARLOS refers to DON JUAN's father:

Don Luis de Tenorio	DAWN LOO-_EESS_
	DAY TEN-_OH_-REE-OH

In IV,3 DON JUAN uses the expression:

chez moi	SHAY-_MWAH_

And he asks after members of Monsieur Dimanche's household:

Claudine	CLOH-_DEEN_
Alphonse	AL-_FAW(N)SS_
Brusquet	BRUH-_SKAY_

In IV,7 SGANARELLE calls for a bottle of:
armagnac AHR-MAN-_YAK_

and DON JUAN refers to a wine:
chablis SHA-_BLEE_

ACKNOWLEDGMENTS

Thanks first to Joan DeJean, who brought this play, its ideas and its checkered history to me in a blaze of excitement and high-octane intellectual curiosity. Her passion for excavation was infectious, and her provocative scholarship grounded me throughout the process of translation and, if you will, reconstruction.

Thanks to Sharon Ott, who commissioned this version of the play for the Seattle Repertory Theatre, for her patience and amused loyalty to me and my theatrical notions. Thanks to the staff of the Seattle Rep, who negotiated this script into being over a shockingly long period, and to Emily Mann, Mara Isaacs and Jeff Woodward of the McCarter Theatre (in 2002), co-producers of the first production and contributors to the development of the script.

Thanks always to Janice Paran, my editor and teacher, whose rigor and wisdom have become reflexes in my mind. And to Mary Birnbaum, who also helped immeasurably with planning, editing, research, and points of translation. Vivienne Chen's sharp eye, bristling intellect, and computer prowess have finally brought the book into being.

I am grateful to the actors who have continued to play this script and whose bracing intelligence has refined it, particularly Adam Stein and Jeremy Webb (Don Juan), Cameron Folmar, Andrew Weems and Michael Milligan (Sganarelle), Francesca Faridany (Donna Elvira/Don Alonso) and Frank Corrado, who was the first to speak the prologue. Thanks Kate Wilson, for your brilliant work with voice and language, which so illuminated the possibilities of this text. Thanks to Jack O'Brien, mentor and pal, who hosted us at the Old Globe in San Diego, and to Michael Kahn, for the invitation to play the Shakespeare Theatre in Washington, and for his generosity while we were there.

I'm grateful to my designers, Kevin Rupnik (sets), Amy Appleyard and later Joan Arhelger (lights), but especially, vis à vis the script, to Anna Oliver (costumes), who worked with me during the writing: we went through thousands of fabric swatches looking for the people in the play as much as for the clothes they might wear in our production.

Rachel Katz-Carey, Lauren Lovett, Miles Markus and Lina Patel and Ophélie Wolf were excellent readers and researchers.

Thanks to Chris Bennion, Susie Cordon, Greg Downer, Charlie Erickson, Stephen Fried, Stephanie Gatton, Marta Johnson, Jerry Manning, Shannon Mills, Elizabeth Monteleone, Bruce Ostler, Craig Schwartz, Virginia Scott, Joseph Smelser, Christine Sumption, Richard Termine, Gary Tucker, the superb Lionel Gossman and—once again, very appreciatively, for their enthusiasm and *patience*—to Marisa Smith and Eric Kraus.

Finally to the Juilliard School, thank you for the 2009 Erskine Faculty Prize, which supported the making of this book.

Stephen Wadsworth